Kay

CHRIST AND THE COSMOS

With love and
many thanks for
your enthusiastic
support.

Gordon

ALSO BY GORDON STRACHAN

available from Labarum Publications Ltd

THE PENTECOSTAL THEOLOGY OF EDWARD IRVING
FREEING THE FEMININE (with Elspeth Strachan)
PROPHETS OF NATURE (forthcoming)

Christ and the Cosmos

GORDON STRACHAN

Labarum Publications Ltd
Dunbar

Labarum Publications Ltd

The Abbey, Dunbar, East Lothian, EH42 1JP

Scotland

ISBN 0 948095 07 5

Typeset by
Pennart Typesetting (Edinburgh) Ltd, Edinburgh, Scotland

Printed and bound in Great Britain by
Thomson Litho Ltd, East Kilbride, Scotland

CONTENTS

v

ILLUSTRATIONS

(Grateful acknowlegements for permission to reproduce the following illustrations is hereby given; uncredited illustrations are by John A. Williams.)

*FOR
MARYEL*

PREFACE

One of the most enjoyable things about taking a sabbatical is the chance to catch up on the reading you promised yourself you would do one day; to have the time to browse through all the fascinating literature you have collected over the years; to do your own free-range study, and to think your own thoughts.

I took such a sabbatical, and found it far too short. Even months of uninterrupted leisure were not enough to grapple with all the exciting and unsettling ideas which seemed to leap out at me from the pages of disparate tomes. I therefore decided, first, to extend my sabbatical and second, to note down all the thoughts which came to me while I read. This book is the result.

I have to confess that I have written a strange and somewhat disturbing book and that, to a certain degree, I am apologetic about it. I feel as though it should perhaps carry a government health warning, or a disclaimer to the effect that the views expressed in it are not necessarily those of the author! Some will think it only proves how dangerous it is to take a sabbatical, because obviously the devil finds work for idle minds to do. Others will see it as clear evidence of mental instability.

To all such, and indeed to my own more orthodox self, I would like to say that this is not the book I meant to write. This is the book that got written – a very different matter. I can say in all honesty that I set out to write about the Bible's attitude to nature: "the Lord's my shepherd", "consider the lilies of the field" and such like. It was all going to be pleasantly pastoral. But the more I allowed the Bible itself to talk to me, the more I found myself looking through nature to the cosmos. I came to see that what we call nature was understood by biblical writers only as the terrestrial part of a cosmology which embraced the whole of the known universe. In so doing I found myself inevitably led into the examination of such taboo subjects as numerology, sacred geometry and astronomy-astrology.

I did not deliberately set out to get involved in such suspect disciplines; it just happened that way. Biblical cosmology is like that. It is all about geometric proportions, the cycles of the heavenly bodies, and numbers. I'm sorry that it should be so. It upsets me to have to accept it. I would much rather it were otherwise, because I do not want to be thought of as a pariah for having drawn attention to certain unacceptable aspects of holy writ. However, that is the risk I must take, since it was these "unpresentable parts" that "found me" in the course of my studies.

Who knows, there may be some (and the winds of change in biblical studies suggest that they are not so few) who will feel that I have stumbled into an area which is of considerable importance for our faith and for our time. They may therefore also, like me, wish to invest these "unpresentable parts" with "the greater honour". In which case the risks I have taken will have been well worthwhile.

If I were to carry my apologetic disclaimer further, I would blame certain friends for having first encouraged me to trespass in these forbidden territories. I would say it was all their fault and that I was led astray by their infectious enthusiasm. However, that would be cowardly and ungrateful. I will instead be courageous and gladly honour my mentors.

It is impossible adequately to thank all those to whom in one way or another I am deeply indebted. Among the cosmologists I have been particularly fortunate to enjoy the inspiration and encouragement of Maryel Gardyne, Anne MacAulay and George Fraser. Without their knowledge and help, this book would not have been completed. Among the astrologers I would especially like to thank Elizabeth Mackintosh and Eileen Foulner for introducing me to the subject and Nicholas Grier, Anne Gardner and Ian Campbell for valuable comments on the manuscript.

The members of my Extra-Mural class at Edinburgh University were stimulating critics, among whom I am most grateful to Peter Gowans for his indefatigable help with numerous points of exegetical detail and to Mark Ferguson for checking my mathematical calculations. Also, among academics, I am greatly indebted to Peter Hayman for many critical comments in the early stages and to John Gibson for kindly reading the final draft and warning me of the wrath to come!

There is another group of friends without whom my wife and I could not have survived. After all, sabbaticals have to be paid for. These were a number of benefactors who wish to remain anonymous, who gave us generous financial support. There were others through whose good offices we received substantial gifts from private trusts. Among these we shall be eternally thankful to Sheila Erdal, Lorna St Aubyn and Cecilia Russell.

There were others whose encouragement came at a particularly crucial moment: I would like to thank Keith Critchlow for his positive vetting of the sacred geometry chapters, and Frank Gosling, Ian MacPhail, Paul Turner and Robin Rae for cheering me on. My thanks go also to Sheila Barnes for her obliging and skilful transformation of my scrappy longhand into faultless typescript.

Any one who is prepared to take the risk of publishing a manuscript such as this commands my deepest respect – and sympathy. For his enthusiasm and drive in this daring adventure I have boundless admiration for my publisher Clive Rawlins.

It is customary to end acknowledgments with suitable praise of one's wife without whose help, patience, understanding . . . etc. I do not demur at such sentiments, I only wish to add that Elspeth and I took our sabbatical together and have already published one book, under joint authorship. We have studied together and have shared all our writing to the point of exhaustion. The only reason why she is not joining me in this authorship is that she does not want to be identified publicly with the lunatic fringe!

CHAPTER 1

THE NEW JERUSALEM AND THE COSMOS

This book is an enquiry into the links between the Bible and ancient cosmology. By cosmology I mean the way in which biblical writers viewed the universe and how it affected their faith in God. I believe that there are aspects of this cosmology in the scriptures which have been neglected by historic Christianity to such an extent that many do not even know they are there.

It is of supreme importance that we rediscover them in these anxious times. The majority of Christians believe in Christ as their personal Saviour and as the head of the Church, but they do not seriously believe he has much to do with the universe as a whole. The gap between a church-centred religion and a cosmic one is enormous and has had tragic consequences, for it is this which has done much to exacerbate the current eco-crisis and threat of nuclear holocaust. It has made God seem far too small to cope with the major ecological issues of our day and has separated Christians from the cosmos.

More than this, there is an apocalyptic side of Christianity which hastens the nuclear catastrophe because it believes that the world will not end with a whimper but a bang. Millenarian fundamentalism which emphasises this aspect of the faith has aided ecological irresponsibility down the centuries. After all, if the world is going to end tomorrow, why bother to be good stewards of creation today? A current example of this can be seen in the U.S.A. in the growth of a protest movement against the assembly of nuclear missiles at Pantex,

Amarillo, Texas, and the "White Train" that transports them around America. Apart from a small group of Christians who have started the peace group "Agape", most of the town's 80 per cent of fundamentalists are very much in favour of nuclear war – for theological reasons:

> Car stickers in Amarillo reveal that attitudes towards Pantex and the White Train are mostly favourable. One sticker I saw said: "I hate Russians". Another announced: "In the event of the Rapture this car will become unmanned".
>
> "The Rapture" is a phenomenon associated with the Second Coming of Christ, which many people in Amarillo believe to be imminent. Christ will appear and summon the faithful to meet him in the air. Many believe that a nuclear holocaust will be a prelude to the Rapture and that the manufacture of nuclear weapons is therefore part of God's plan.[1]

Even many moderate Christians who would feel they had little in common with such extreme fundamentalists, hardly differ from them in their general pessimism about the long-term future. At best it would seem that a form of blinkered agnosticism, a whistling in the dark, is about as much hope as most church people have for posterity.

I believe that a rediscovery of the cosmic dimension of Christianity will help us find a genuine hope for the future which will replace our pessimistic forebodings with real optimism. It will help us to realise that it is not the *world* which is about to end, as so many believe, but the *age*. This enquiry I believe, will inspire confidence by helping us to see the horrendous signs of our times as the death throes of one cosmic age and the birth-pangs of another.

The key texts for my belief in the cosmic dimension of Christianity and of Christ himself are taken from the writings of St Paul where he speaks of Jesus as the one "through whom all things exist" (1*Cor.* 8:6) and as the one through whom God has chosen "to unite all things

. . . things in heaven and things on earth" (*Eph.* 1:10). St Paul is making the point that it is not just the Church that exists through Christ, it is also all things, *ta panta*, by which he means the whole of creation. This is stated even more clearly in *Colossians* 1:15-17:

> He [Jesus Christ] is the image of the invisible God, the first-born of all creation; for in him all things were created, in heaven and on earth, visible and invisible, whether thrones or dominions or principalities or authorities – all things were created through him and for him. He is before all things, and in him all things hold together.

This New Testament belief in Christ as the creator of all things, the *pantocrator* as the early Church called him, is not unique to St Paul. St John, in the prologue to his gospel, calling Christ "the Word", *logos*, says much the same:

> In the beginning was the Word, and the Word was with God, and the Word was God. He was in the beginning with God; all things were made through him, and without him was not anything made that was made.

These are tremendous and unassailable statements of the belief that Jesus Christ made all things. I want to take such texts as the authorisation for my enquiry and go on to examine their staggering implications. What does it really mean that Christ created all things? Surely one of the things it must imply is that everything belongs to him. All created things must therefore in a sense be precious, even holy. Such a realisation should encourage us to have what Albert Schweitzer called a "reverence for life". How then can we be in any way in favour of the nuclear arms race or the ecological devastation of the planet? If "all things were made through him" – and indeed were redeemed through him – then the implication is that all things are worth conserving and not meant to be destroyed.

3

In this study we shall be looking at passages through-out the Bible which support and enlarge upon these basic texts. We shall start at the end of the scriptures, in the last two chapters of the *Revelation*, since it is *Revelation* which has been used more than any other book in the Bible to justify an apocalyptic world view.[2] It is here that we shall find our first surprise – that the vision of the New Jerusalem does not describe a heavenly town, as has been traditionally understood, but a cosmic paradise descend-ing *from* heaven *to* earth. Jesus Christ is, in fact, pictured as the Lamb of God with his Father in the centre of a model of the cosmos. When we understand St John's symbolism, this will become very clear.

The Cosmic Cube

The shape of the New Jerusalem is a perfect cube, for St John says "The city lies foursquare . . . its length and breadth and height are equal" (*Rev.* 21:16). It could perhaps have been a pyramid, thus offering a convenient downflow for the river of life, as one ingenious scholar suggests,[3] but this is unlikely because pyramids were never associated with the Jews, always with the Egyptians.[4] How could a city be in the shape of a cube, especially one 1,500 miles, "twelve thousand stadia" (*Rev.* 21:16), in length, breadth and height? It would be some city!

Most commentators solve this riddle by agreeing that both the shape and size of the city must be taken as symbolic. Some go on to claim that this is St John's version of then current Jewish ideas about the vast cubic city "exalted on high up to the darkening clouds",[5] which God would raise up out of the ashes of the Roman destruction of Jerusalem in 70 A.D.[6] But such specula-tions raise the question as to whether the New Jerusalem is meant to be understood, even symbolically, as a city in the usual sense of the word. Its extraordinary shape and size might lead us to wonder whether the word *polis*, city, may not be used here to mean something rather different. Reading Lewis Mumford's classic *The City in History* I came across just such another meaning which seemed to fit St John's possible intention much better. This was the earliest understanding of *polis* which, according to Mumford, was conceived of as a model of the whole cosmos:

> Beginning as a representation of the cosmos, a means of bringing heaven down to earth, the city became a symbol of the possible. Utopia was an integral part of its original constitution.[7]

This picture of the city as a "representation of the cosmos" is very like St John's vision, for he says on two occasions that he saw the holy city "coming down out of heaven from God" (*Rev.* 21:2, 10) in much the same way as Mumford speaks of the original ideal of the city being conceived of as "a means of bringing heaven down to earth". Elsewhere Mumford elaborates on this interpretation, this time calling the city a "man-made replica of the universe" which "opened an attractive vista: indeed a glimpse of heaven itself". He then goes on to describe the ideal life of this cosmic city "within sight of the Gods and their king",[8] in remarkably similar terms to St John's visionary voice: "Behold, the dwelling of God is with men. He will dwell with them, and they shall be his people; and God himself will be with them" (*Rev.* 21: 3-4). I believe that it is highly likely that St John did mean the New Jerusalem to be understood as a representation of the cosmos as much as of the Church and as a replica of the universe as much as the future home of the elect.

This cosmic interpretation would certainly explain in what way the cube was meant to be symbolic – a question which has continually foxed scholars. Most of them agree that it is a symbol of perfection[9] and some go on to say that it symbolised perfect symmetry[10] but only M. R.

Newbolt, to my knowledge, in *The Book of Unveiling* offers an explanation as to why this should be so. He links the cube with the geometric and numerical philosophy associated with Pythagoras:

> To the Greeks (and St John lived in a Hellenized world) geometry had a fascination; to Pythagoras, an Asiatic Greek, number was identical with all that is orderly, proper, right, good and beautiful. Its clearness and certainty demonstrated the power of reason over the formless and unpredictable world of the senses.[11]

Pythagoras was, of course, not merely "an Asiatic Greek" with a peculiar penchant for numbers. He was one of the greatest thinkers of the ancient world and is widely regarded as the founding father of Western philosophy and science. Yet, as recent scholarship has shown, he was only the mouthpiece for a cosmology of number and geometry which was prevalent throughout the whole of the Middle East many centuries before he lived. Otto Neugebauer, in *The Exact Sciences in Antiquity*, for example, shows that in the third millennium BC. the Babylonians knew all about "reciprocals, multiplications, squares and square roots, cubes and cube roots, the sums of squares and cubes, . . . exponential functions, coefficients giving numbers for practical computation . . . and numerous metrological calculations giving the area of rectangles, circles", etc. The famous theorem of Pythagoras was known in Babylon "more than a thousand years before Pythagoras".[12] Therefore, slighting though Newbolt's reference is, I nevertheless believe him to be right in suggesting the connection between the cube and Pythagoreanism.

The most famous and influential disciple of Pythagoras was Plato. In the *Timaeus*, he links the four elements out of which the ancients believed the whole world to be constructed, to four regular geometric solids.[13] These were the tetrahedron which was used to represent the element of fire, the octahedron which represented air, the icosahedron which represented water and the cube which represented earth.

Let us assign the cube to earth; for it is the most immobile of the four bodies and the most retentive of shape, and these are characteristics that must belong to the figure with the most stable faces.[14]

Here we appear to have a problem because if St John was following the Platonic tradition, his cube should only have symbolised the earth and not the cosmos. If he had been a true Platonist his cosmos would have to have been represented by Plato's "fifth construction, which the god used for embroidering the constellations on the whole heaven".[15] This fifth regular geometric solid which represented the cosmos is usually taken to have been the twelve-faced dodecahedron.

The answer to this apparent discrepancy lies in the fact that Plato did not explicitly state that the dodecahedron was the representation of the cosmos. It was only the four regular solids that he did specify as being used in practical cosmology. The cube therefore came to represent the cosmos as well as the earth because the other three solids were traditionally constructed geometrically within it. Thus the cube of earth, containing all the other elements of the created universe, fire, air and water, was held to contain the cosmos. A variation of this can be seen as late as the seventeenth century in Kepler's model of the solar system. We may say therefore that it was most likely that St John was influenced by this tradition and, lest we should worry that we might on that account have to accept him as a crypto-Platonist, let me stress that the geometric cosmology which Plato got from Pythagoras can be found in the temples, ziggurats and pyramids

1 Kepler's model of the solar system

throughout the ancient world.[16] St John was using the symbolism not so much of "an Asiatic Greek" as of an apparently universal cosmology which predated the earliest Greek philosophers by at least a thousand years.

This tradition of a cubic universe is only implicit in the Bible but does surface explicitly in the third century A.D. Jewish mystical document *The Book of Creation*, the *Sefer Yesira*. In a recent translation, the cosmos is specifically likened to a cube:

8

Twelve edges of a cube, divided into six faces, separated in each direction . . . And they expand continually for ever and ever, and they are the arms of the universe.[17]

This is a powerful piece of evidence in confirmation of the cosmic significance of the cubic shape of the New Jerusalem. It also has a strangely modern ring to it for it almost seems to look like an earlier version of the contemporary astronomical theory of the expanding universe, which has been so much in the news in recent years. Carl Sagan in *Cosmos* notes the similarity between certain aspects of Hindu cosmology and the "Steady State" theory, but fails to notice just as startling a similarity between this expanding cubic universe of ancient Jewish mysticism and the so-called "Big Bang" theory. Had he done so he would have drawn our attention to the peculiar likeness of these two theories when he was endeavouring to explain the mysteries of the fourth dimension by means of a tesseract or hypercube. Although he said he could not show us a tesseract because we are trapped in three-dimensional space, he said he could show us its shadow in three dimensions: "It resembles two nested cubes, all the vertices connected by lines".[18] Then, on the basis of this definition, he goes on to explain the theory of the expanding universe.

2 *Sagan's model of a tesseract*

9

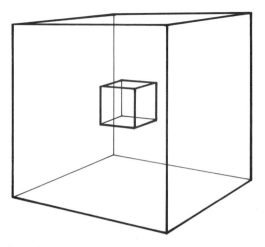

3 New Jerusalem as a transparent cube

If we compare Sagan's model of a tesseract or hypercube with that of the New Jerusalem as a transparent cube within a cubic universe, the two are found to be identical, for both are nested cubes. The holy city as a paradigm of the cosmos may yet find some friends among modern astro-physicists!

The Foundation Jewels as the Signs of the Zodiac

If we turn from the shape to the foundations of the New Jerusalem, an equally universal symbol can be seen. St John tells us that "The foundations of the city were adorned with every jewel" (*Rev.* 21:19) and these jewels are listed in full (*Rev.* 21:19 – 20). Scholars have often wondered why all the individual names of the jewels were given and have generally concluded that they are symbolic of the twelve signs of the zodiac.[19] But following R.H. Charles' interpretation of Athanasius Kircher,[20] they have been anxious to point out that the list of constellations is given in "exactly the reverse order of the actual path of the sun through the signs",[21] and this they attribute to St John's "polemical motive".[22] In spite of admitting an obvious link between the jewels and the stones in the High Priest's breast-plate and that these stones were taken by both Philo and Josephus as symbolic of the zodiac, they still contend with Charles that "this order is deliberately adopted by John and is intended as a repudiation of the pagan association of the Zodiac".[23]

Such has been the traditional Christian taboo against astrology that few writers have dared to question this position. Among those who have, G. R. Beasley-Murray stands out as particularly courageous. Commenting on the pervasive view that St John is "not giving a Christianized version of the 'city of the gods' of pagan speculation",[24] he says: "This is doubtful, for the connection is too striking for a rejection to be communicated in this way". He then goes on to say that he believes that this Christianising of pagan speculation is precisely what St John is doing:

> It is more likely that John's listing of the jewel signs *plus his connecting them with the people of God and apostles of the Lamb* is intended to suggest that *the reality after which the pagans aspire is found in the revelation of God in Jesus Christ.*[25]

Earlier, referring to the shape and size of the New Jerusalem he makes this position even clearer:

> John unhesitatingly appropriated for the city of God ideas relating to the city of the stars which were beloved by the pagan astrologers of his day . . . John declares that the reality which corresponds to their imperfect vision is to be found in the city of God and of the Lamb.[26]

I confess that I find this interpretation much more convincing than that of Charles and his followers. I agree

11

with Beasley-Murray that the connection between the jewels and the zodiac is "too striking for a rejection to be communicated in this way". I believe that St John was painting a picture of a Christ who was not just head of the Church but who was also the Lord of the farthest bounds of the universe. Scholars have been too quick to deny this astrological dimension; in so doing they have also tended to deny Christ's lordship over his creation. St John's symbolism shows the Lamb on his throne in the midst of his created universe. I believe that Austin Farrar is also correct when he boldly states that the New Jerusalem "is a four-square city embracing the whole zodiac".[27]

Further unprejudiced research along these lines confirms this positive link between astrology and the early Judeo-Christian tradition. For instance J. Massyng-berde Ford has no difficulty in proving it archaeologically:

> The signs of the zodiac are depicted in mosaics in synagogues in Palestine, indicating the Jews felt no incongruity in adopting these pagan signs and linking them with Jewish ideas.[28]

More evidence that the Kircher-Charles hegemony may not stand up much longer to unblinkered scholarship comes from J. C. Cooper's *An Illustrated Encyclopaedia of Traditional Symbols*, where in her entry under "Zodiac"[29] she lists the jewels which in her view correspond to each of the signs. It is extraordinary to note that her list is almost the exact *opposite* of Kircher, Charles and company. The fact that she does not connect her list in any way with the New Jerusalem makes it all the more remarkable. We might parody Charles' famous comment and say "this cannot be an accident". In all except chrysolite and chrysoprase, Cooper's list is exactly the same as St John's – with no reverse order.

Zodiac	Kircher-Charles & Co.	Cooper	St John
Aries	amethyst	diamond	jasper (diamond - Jerusalem Bible)
Taurus	jacinth	sapphire	sapphire
Gemini	chrysoprase	agate	agate
Cancer	topaz	emerald	emerald
Leo	beryl	sardonyx	sardonyx
Virgo	chrysolite	cornelian	cornelian
Libra	carnelian	opal and lapis lazuli	chrysolite
Scorpio	sardonyx	beryl	beryl
Sagittarius	emerald	topaz	topaz
Capricorn	chalcedony	jet and black onyx	chrysoprase
Aquarius	sapphire	zircon	jacinth (a type of zircon)
Pisces	jasper	amethyst	amethyst

Enough has now been said to show that much traditional Christian scholarship has been at pains to deny the cosmic significance of the New Jerusalem and by implication also to deny the cosmic rule of the Lamb on his throne. This tradition must now be regarded as biased and detrimental to the cause of the one in whom "all things hold together" (*Col.* 1:17).

The Gates as the Portals of the Moon

Moving on now from the foundations to the gates of the city, we encounter the same anti-cosmic prejudice in most commentators who either see the pearls – "the twelve gates were twelve pearls" (*Rev.* 21:21) – as a reference to the pearl of great price (*Matt.* 13:46) or who, once again influenced by Charles, [30] assert that St John is following a rabbinic tradition that God would one day bring "pearls thirty cubits long by thirty cubits broad . . . and they shall stand in the gates of Jerusalem".[31] This is predictable but disappointing, because had Charles been open to a more positive view of the possible link between St John's symbolism and "ethnic speculations regarding the city of the gods" he would perhaps have seen a parallel between the twelve gates of the city and the twelve "portals" or "gates" of the heavens through which the sun, moon and stars were believed to rise and set in the sky. These he himself elucidates at length in his own classic commentary on the *Book of Enoch*, telling us in detail where to look for the different kinds of portals:

Cf XXXIII – XXXVI for portals of winds and stars. In LXXII – LXXXII, sun, moon and stars pass through the same portals, but in XXXIII – XXXVI the stars' portals are small, while in LXXII one of the sun's portals is called 'great'.[32]

Alas, there is no lateral thinking in Charles or his disciples. The only scholar who, to my knowledge, accepts this link is William Barclay in *The Daily Study Bible* where he speaks of the "twelve gates through which the stars went in and out upon their business".[33] If with Barclay we were to accept this gate-portal connection, then J. C. Cooper's interpretation of pearl symbolism becomes most intriguing. She says that the pearl is pre-eminently a lunar symbol. It represents the moon above all things.[34] Would it be reasonable to suggest that the twelve gates-which-are-pearls might well symbolise the twelve "portals" of the moon and thus the twelve months of the year? If so, quite apart from representing the "twelve tribes of the sons of Israel" (*Rev.* 21:12) and possibly the pearl of great price, they might also speak of the lordship of the Lamb over time in the same way as the jewel-zodiac-foundations speak of his lordship over space.

The Street as the Milky Way

This "portals of the moon" interpretation would also be

consistent with Beasley-Murray when he suggests that "the street of the city" (*Rev.* 21:21) was not some oriental high street but was nothing less than the highway of the stars. He makes the claim that "the model for the street is none other than the Milky Way".[35] Barclay once more agrees, saying that "the Milky Way was its great street."[36]

The Eden Centre

We have succeeded in finding a cosmic meaning for the cubic shape, the foundations, gates and street of the holy city. What about its contents? What actually is inside? Scholars speak of its gate-towers and numerous streets; hymn writers from Augustine to Samuel Johnson wax eloquent over its halls, houses, turrets and pinnacles[37] and artists from Hans Lufft illustrating Luther's Bible to Annie Vallotton in *Today's English Version* show it

4   *Hans Lufft's New Jerusalem*

crammed full of the same urban features. But where are all these splendid civic amenities to be found in the text? Where does St John speak of streets in the plural (*plateia* is singular)?[38] Where does he mention gate-*towers* or any towers for that matter? Where does he describe any halls, houses, turrets or pinnacles? The answer to all these questions is, of course, that he doesn't make a single reference to any of them. They simply cannot be found. All of them are inferences from the misconceived notion that by "city" St John meant a metropolis. We have seen that the evidence against this urban meaning is considerable, and when we examine what the text does say was actually in the city it becomes overwhelming. St John makes it quite clear that the only things inside the walls, apart from the street already referred to, are the throne of God and the Lamb, the river of the water of life, and the tree of life (*Rev.* 22:1 – 2):

> Then he showed me the river of the water of life, bright as crystal, flowing from the throne of God and of the Lamb through the middle of the street of the city; also on either side of the river, the tree of life with its twelve kinds of fruit, yielding its fruit each month; and the leaves of the tree were for the healing of the nations.

Whatever the river and the tree of life were meant to symbolise, one thing is certain – they were not images of a conurbation. How they were ever thought to be so is almost inexplicable. Once we change our preconceptions from an ecclesiastical town to an image of the cosmos, then the meaning of the symbolism becomes obvious. St John's vision was of a "new heaven *and* a new earth" (*Rev.* 21:1). So far, all the details we have examined have been found to be symbolic of the heavens. Here at last we have been given symbols of the earth. I fail to see what meaning can be given to the river of the water of life and the tree of life other than that of an earthly rural paradise. They are so reminiscent of the story of the garden of Eden (*Gen.* 2:9–10) that I believe they must be taken as the ecological equivalent of all that has been said so far about cosmology. St John is telling us that the Lamb on his

16

throne is Lord also of a new earth order in which harmony will be restored as at the beginning. Thus the Bible not only begins, but also ends with a garden. This is of paramount importance for the Green Movement today as it seeks to deschool Western technological man from the false belief that progress consists in abandoning rural roots in favour of larger and larger cities.

5 Annie Vallotton's New Jerusalem

Crystal Consciousness

Having now completed this cosmic and ecological interpretation of the New Jerusalem, it only remains to offer some explanation for the crystalline nature of the whole structure. St John says that it had "radiance like a most rare jewel, like a jasper, clear as crystal" (*Rev.* 21:11). He also says "The wall was built of jasper, while the city was built of pure gold, clear as glass" (*Rev.* 21:18). All of this suggests that the whole edifice was made of crystal, not just the foundations. This would agree with the basic physics of crystal shapes, of which a prominent one is the cube, as anyone who chooses to examine this branch of science can confirm.[39] Beyond the scientific authenticity of cubic crystals there has in recent years been a resurgence of interest in the powerful psychic and spiritual properties of crystals.

17

What could be described as a crystal-mysticism has grown up as an aspect of current developments in complementary medicine. Crystal is thought of in these circles as a symbol of the spirit.The "state of transparency" is reckoned to be the manifestation of the harmonious union of opposites because it is matter which exists, yet seems not to exist. It is solid, yet also transparent. Mellie Uyldert in *The Magic of Precious Stones* has absorbing chapters on the differing powers of gems and their link with astrology, religion and healing;[40] Ra Bonewitz also develops the latter aspect in *Cosmic Crystals, Crystal Consciousness and the New Age*. His chapters on crystal energies and personal and planetary healing through crystals, raise fundamental questions about the links between modern crystallography and ancient mysticism. As a scientist as well as a mystic, Bonewitz believes that reality inhabits neither the material nor the spiritual in its entirety but "dwells equally in both".[41] He goes so far as to say that it is this concept of the marriage of matter and spirit which has given birth to this most arresting book. His use of the metaphor of marriage in this connection once again points us back to the holy city which St John describes as being "prepared as a bride adorned for her husband" (*Rev.* 21:2) and as "the Bride, the wife of the Lamb" (*Rev.* 21:9). The New Jerusalem as the Bride, the wife of the Lamb, does seem to fit the idea of the union of opposites, matter and spirit, of which Bonewitz and others speak. This is equally the case in his comments about planetary healing for St John says that "the leaves of the tree were for the healing of the nations" (*Rev.* 22:2).

In *The World Atlas of Mysteries*, Francis Hitching speaks of three Russian scientists in the 1960s who came to believe through their researches, that planet earth was originally and is still essentially crystalline. In the chapter "Crystalline Planet"[42] he summarises their contention that our world is constructed out of 12 pentagonal slabs

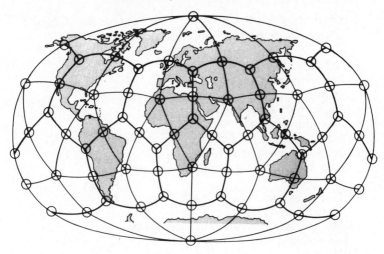

6 *Crystalline planet*

which cover the globe and thus make it a dodecahedron. This takes us back to Plato, who said "the real earth viewed from above is supposed to look like one of those balls made out of twelve pieces of skin sewn together".[43] Whether or not this Russian theory is true, it is interesting to speculate on the possibility. Was the earth originally a crystalline dodecahedron? St John is quite clear that the unity of heaven and earth in the crystal of the New Jerusalem symbolises the mystical marriage between Christ and his creation. Bonewitz reminds us that "crystal is a perfect expression of the divine mind . . . When you tune in to the energy of the crystal, you are tuning in to a very precise aspect of the divine mind".[44] Whether in the microcosm or the macrocosm it seems crystals can still communicate something of the message that came to St John. It is still a message for healing, not for disease, for harmony not discord, for revelation not apocalypse.

As I read Bonewitz and Hitching I couldn't help

remembering Milton's *Ode on the Morning of Christ's Nativity*. It seemed to take on a new meaning:

Ring out, ye crystal spheres!
Once bless our human ears,
If you have power to touch our senses so;
And let your silver chime
Move in melodious time;
And let the base of Heaven's deep organ blow;
And with your ninefold harmony
Make up full consort to the angelic symphony.

For if such holy song
Enwrap your fancy long,
Time will run back, and fetch the age of gold;
And speckled vanity
Will sicken soon and die,
And leprous sin will melt from earthly mould;
And Hell itself will pass away,
And leave her dolorous mansions to the peering day.

(Further examination of the New Jerusalem can be found in the Appendix.)

CHAPTER 2

THE TEMPLE AND THE COSMOS

The cubic shape of the New Jerusalem is modelled on the Holy of Holies in Solomon's temple, where we are told "The inner sanctuary was twenty cubits long, twenty cubits wide and twenty cubits high" (*1 Kings* 6:20). St John saw the whole city "as itself the Holy of Holies"[1] vastly magnified. It had all become holy because "Christ has destroyed the veil of separation which kept men out and has opened a new and living way by which all are invited to approach".[2]

If we examine the architectural proportions of the temple, as given in the Old Testament, we shall find that, even in the tenth century B.C., the same geometric and numerical cosmology is evident as in the New Jerusalem. Nigel Pennick, in his chapter on the Hebrews in *Sacred Geometry*, explains the ancient belief that the little world or microcosm of the holy buildings was supposed to correspond in every detail to the macrocosm of the universe:

As a microcosm, it was necessary that the temple or tabernacle should directly reflect in its dimensions, geometry and orientation, the conditions and structure of the macrocosm of which it was at once an image and a means of direct access. Indeed Josephus asserts that 'this proportion of the measures of the Tabernacle (*or temple*) proved to be an imitation of the system of the world'.[3]

21

The Musical Measures of the Temple

The question still remains, why was the cosmos imagined to be a cube? We have already answered this in part by saying that it was held to contain the other three platonic solids and the elements which they represented. Pennick however gives another reason which relates the Holy of Holies in the temple directly to the New Jerusalem: "the symbolic cube . . . like the City of Revelation or the Jewish Holy of Holies, contains the consonances of the Universe".[4] Pennick is here referring to yet another important dimension of the ancient wisdom, namely the link between architectural proportion and the ratios of musical notes. For the ancient world – not just Pythagoras – all things were numbers and all numbers had correspondences in every area of knowledge. The cube was symbolic of all the consonances in music because the ratios of all its sides are 1:1. The ratio of 1:1 in music represents the note of unison or the full string-length and the full string-length contains within itself the vibrations

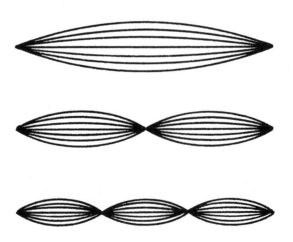

7 The musical intervals of string vibrations

of all the other musical intervals. These notes within the full string-length are known as "overtones", as Percy Scholes describes:

> The string simultaneously vibrates as a whole and also in two and three equal parts, respectively (and also of course, in other smaller parts). Its vibration as a whole produces the fundamental note; in halves the note an octave higher; and in thirds the note a twelfth higher – and so on with the smaller simultaneous divisions not shown here.[5]

The cube was the architectural equivalent of the full string-length – the fundamental – and was thus held to contain the whole of the overtone series, ie. all the consonances of the universe. Guy Murchie in *Music of the Spheres* adds yet another harmonic analogy to the sacredness of the cube in ancient cosmology. This was to do with the ratio of its faces and edges to its points: "Even the abstract cube was held sacred because its eight corners form the harmonic mean between its six faces and its twelve edges."[6] In other words, if twelve is the fundamental and six the octave, then eight is the dominant fifth.

This musical interpretation of the proportions of the Holy of Holies applied equally to the other larger but less sacred chamber of the temple, the Holy Place, as can be demonstrated by analysing its proportions along the same lines. We are told that the overall size of these two adjacent chambers was "sixty cubits long, twenty cubits wide and thirty cubits high" (*1 Kings* 6:2). This building was then partitioned off at twenty cubits to make the inner sanctuary, the Holy of Holies. So "the nave in front of the inner sanctuary was forty cubits long" (*1 Kings* 6:17). Thus the proportions of the Holy Place were 40 x 30 x 20 cubits. If these are divided by their highest common factor, 10, they become 4 x 3 x 2. If these are then put into three sets of ratios, they become 1 to 2 (the same as 2 to 4), 2 to 3, and 3 to 4. As fractions, these ratios are ½, ⅔ and ¾. It is an extraordinary fact that these ratios and fractions are exactly the same as those which mark the musical intervals of the octave, the fifth and the fourth or, as the Greeks later called them, the diapason, the diapente and the diatessaron.[7]

8 *The ratios of musical intervals*

The Holy Place can therefore be said to have expressed, in ratios of architectural proportion, the same musical tones which were implicit in the unison or fundamental note of the Holy of Holies.

9 *Temple measurements and proportions*

These four notes, the fundamental, the octave, the fifth and the fourth, are known as the perfect consonances because they are invariable. They cannot be changed into the major or minor key and are therefore the very basis of harmony. The other consonances of the scale, the third and the sixth, are thought of as imperfect because they are

24

variable. However, both of these were also built into the construction of the temple because the 40 x 30 cubit rectangles, which formed the two longer sides of the Holy Place, were thought of as two 3:4:5 triangles sharing the same hypotenuse.

10 The 3, 4, 5 triangles in the Holy Place

The 3:4:5 triangle was held to correspond to these two imperfect consonances as well as the fourth because, if the full string-length is taken as corresponding to the hypotenuse of 5 units, then the ratios it forms with the other two sides are 4 to 5 and 3 to 5, and these correspond to the intervals of the major third and the sixth.

11 The musical ratios of the 3, 4, 5 triangle

25

Although there are no explicit biblical references to this musical interpretation of the temple proportions, there are many clues to it implicit in the important role which the Israelites attributed to music in the temple tradition, beginning with King David "the sweet psalmist of Israel"(*2 Sam.* 23:1) who, according to the Chronicler, got the measurements "from the hand of the Lord" (*1 Chron.* 28:11-19). It is particularly intriguing to note in this connection that, in the Chronicler's version of the dedication of the temple, it was when the 288 levitical singers (*1 Chron.*25:7) and the "hundred and twenty priests who were trumpeters" (*2 Chron.* 5:12) "raised the song" to God "in unison" (*2 Chron.* 5:13), that "the house of the Lord, was filled with a cloud" and "the glory of the Lord filled the house of God" (*2 Chron.* 5:14). This is usually taken to be a reference to the cloud which covered Mount Sinai, when God revealed his glory and his law to Moses (*Ex.* 24:15-18). The implication is that Solomon and his people, having obediently built everything "according to the plan", had now found divine approbation. The inner connection between Mount Sinai and the temple was that the latter had been built as a permanent home for the Ark of the Covenant, the box which contained the very tablets of stone on which Moses had originally written the law. But we can now also legitimately interpret this story according to our musical cosmology, for it would fit all that we have discovered about the temple measurements and their correspondence to the consonances of the universe. According to this, the Chronicler would be telling us that the laws of harmony were seen as an expression of the Torah and that the temple, as the architectural embodiment of that harmony, as "frozen music",[8] rang true. The singers and trumpeters chimed perfectly with the harmoniously proportioned building. As they raised their song "in unison", all the consonances in this perfect microcosm would have begun to vibrate. By his own law of correspondence God was bound to answer from the macrocosm.

Having examined the musical measurements of the Holy of Holies and the Holy Place, I would now like to take a close look at the door which connected these two rooms.

The Pentagonal Door

The shape of the door which led into the Holy of Holies is described in the *A.V.* as if it was in breadth, a fifth part of the total part of the chamber, for it says "the lintel and the side posts were a fifth part of the wall" (*1 Kings* 6:31). C. F. Burney, contradicting many earlier scholars who had accepted this, says that this translation is "alien to the context".[9] Although the Hebrew text is admittedly obscure, he suggests that the "fifth part" refers not to the breadth of the wall but to the jambs or side posts of the door itself. James A. Montgomery, following Burney, agrees that the verse describes a "pentagonal doorway, ie. with a peaked roof"[10] and he compares it with a similar door illustrated on a third century coin from Byblos. More recent scholarship agrees with this as, for example, John Gray, who says "hamīšīt ('a fifth') should probably be read hamūšōt ('fivefold') ie. a pentagon".[11]

This scholarly consensus has been reflected in many more recent translations of the Bible. For instance, the *R.S.V.* says "the lintel and the door posts were pentagonal", the *Living Bible*, that the doorway was "a five-sided opening", and the *N.I.V.*, that the doors had "five-sided jambs".

But there still remains an uncertainty as to what exactly the pentagonal door would have looked like. Burney gives a small illustration of a normal door with an angular arch. Other scholars would probably agree with him and with Montgomery who describes the door as having a "peaked roof". This may very well have been the case and,

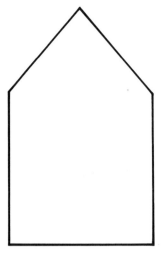

12 Burney's arched door

with the Hebrew text being corrupt, no one will ever know for certain. Nevertheless, in the light of all that has been said so far about the sacred geometry built into Solomon's temple, it would be reasonable to suggest that this door might actually have been built in the shape of an exact pentagon.

13 The pentagonal door

I put this suggestion forward because the pentagon was thought of as one of the most powerful of geometric symbols and therefore would have been a most appropriate shape for such a uniquely important doorway. It would also be consistent with the sacred geometry of the whole building as already described. None of the commentators cited mentions this as a possibility, but then only one of them commenting earlier on the Holy of Holies (1 Kings 6:20) makes even the briefest reference to the fact that it was a cube.[12] Although this is disappointing, it is not surprising because, as we have noted with regard to the New Jerusalem, geometric considerations have been largely neglected by biblical scholars. I make this point to emphasise that, had commentators regarded the cubic shape of the Holy of Holies as important and had they known why, they would most likely have also accepted that this door was in the form of an exact pentagon because they would have seen its symbolic significance. What then was the importance of this symbol and why is it probable that it was the shape of the door into the Holy of Holies?

The number five and hence the pentagon and five-pointed star, the pentagram, were always associated in numerology and geometry with humankind and with perfection. As J. C. Cooper says, it represented "the human microcosm; the number of man. The pentagon, shares the symbolism of the perfection and power of the circle".[13] Robert Lawlor likewise says the pentagon was "the symbol of life, particularly of human life"[14] and gives an illustration of man as the pentagon.

In the ritual of the temple, the high priest, representing the whole nation of Israel, went into the Holy of Holies once a year on the Day of Atonement to obtain expiation for the sins of the people. No one else was ever allowed into this Most Holy Place. He went through the pentagonal door as, so to speak, the pentagramal man, ie. man in the process of being made perfect. The door into

14 Man as the pentagon

the perfect cube of the cosmos had to represent the shape of the perfect man. Although by New Testament times this door had been replaced by a curtain or veil, Christ as perfect high priest "after the order of Melchizedek" (*Heb.* 7:11) entered the Holy of Holies when the "curtain of the temple was torn in two" (*Luke* 23:45). As it says in the letter to the Hebrews:

> But when Christ appeared as a high priest of the good things that have come . . . he entered once and for all into the Holy Place taking . . . his own blood, thus securing an eternal redemption. (*Heb.* 9:11-12)

This connection between the perfect pentagramal man and the perfect pentagonal doorway is brought out by John Michell in his profound study of the links between the temple and the New Jerusalem, *City of Revelation*.

Michell's scholarship is based on the evidence of gematria, another ancient numerical discipline in which every Hebrew and Greek letter corresponded to a number.[15] Speaking about the pentagon-pentagram relationship he makes an astonishing link between it and the gematria of the name of Jesus Christ (in Greek, *Iēsous Christos*):

> There is an obvious connection between the pentagram and the body of the canonical man crucified, which is confirmed in the golden section measurements of the human body, and the following circumstance could scarcely have been ignored by the founders of the Christian religion: that a square drawn on the height of a pentagon with a side measuring one unit has an area of 2.368, and 2368 is the number of the crucified man, Iēsous Christos. In Fig. 23 the horizontal dotted line, approximately coinciding with the upper limbs of the pentagram, divides the square into two rectangles so that the area of the upper rectangle is 888, Jesus, of the lower 1480, Christ.

'Ιησους
0·888

Χριστος
1·480

15 Side of pentagon

That 2368, the most sacred number of the Christian cabalists, the sum of the values of the letter in the name of Jesus Christ, should be a thousand times the area of a square on the height of a pentagon measuring 1 unit on every side is a law of nature and not a contrivance of ancient geometers ... The sacred numbers are not merely from human choice: they are inherent in the structure of the universe and must recur to whoever studies the unifying science of cosmology.[16]

For those who are unfamiliar with the inner rationale of gematria and its geometric correspondences, this passage from Michell will be difficult to understand, let alone evaluate. But for those who have studied this ancient discipline, all that he says will confirm that the pentagon-pentagram represented by the shape of the doorway into the Holy of Holies, was realised in the person and work of Jesus Christ.

The Icons of Eden

It was not only the cubic shape of the New Jerusalem that St John took from the symbolism of the temple. His vision of a restored Eden, as described in chapter 1, was also pictured in terms of its contents, for if we look at the sacred objects and wall carvings that were inside the temple, it is not difficult to see that they were stylised representations of the main features of the garden of Eden.

We are told that for the Holy Place, Solomon made "the golden altar, the golden table for the bread of the Presence, the lampstands of pure gold, five on the south side and five on the north, before the inner sanctuary" (1 Kings 7:48-49). These were usually known as the altar of incense, the table of shewbread and the seven-branch candlesticks. The symbolism of these pieces of holy furniture has been seen by traditional scholarship almost exclusively in spiritual terms; the incense as prayer, the bread as the Bread of Life and the candlesticks as the Light of God.[17] While there is undoubted truth in such interpretations, they entirely obscure the original connection which all these objects had with nature; the gum and resin of incense with the fragrance of the forest,[18] the cereal offering of the shewbread with agricultural production,[19] and the candlesticks with the almond tree (*Ex.* 25:31-40). It is these lampstands which point back most obviously to the garden of Eden because it was the almond tree which was the tree of life for the Hebrews.[20] As St John saw the tree of life standing in the midst of the New Jerusalem, so the Israelites saw an avenue of the same trees of life standing within the temple. In both cases they symbolised an earthly paradise and the message was one of harmony with nature. This is borne out by the clear ecological meaning of Ezekiel's vision of this same avenue of trees coming to life in the desert (*Ezek.* 47:1-12, cf *Rev.* 22:1-2).

The wall decorations of the Holy Place and the Holy of Holies agree with this Edenic interpretation because we are told that Solomon "carved all the walls round about with carved figures of cherubim and palm trees and open flowers in the inner and the outer rooms". (*1 Kings* 6:29). Although the actual appearance of the cherubim is uncertain, scholars agree that they were thought of as God's servants whose main job was to guard "the Tree of Life in the Garden of Eden" (*Gen.* 3:24).[21] This understanding of the cherubim as "guardians of Paradise"[22] is developed by John Gray with specific reference to the temple wall carvings where he says "they guard the palm-tree as the tree of life",[23] the date-palm being the tree of life for the nomads of the desert in the same way as the almond tree was for the Jews.[24]

There was nothing else in the temple except what it had been specifically built to house – the Ark of the Covenant. This box containing the Law stood in the centre of the Holy of Holies flanked by its two enormous protecting cherubim. In terms of our Eden imagery this symbolised the living presence of the Lord God in the midst of his creation (*Gen.* 3:8).

As the structure of the temple expressed the perfect harmony of the cosmos in architectural proportions equivalent to those of the pure musical intervals, so its contents expressed the same universal harmony in its earthly form of the trees, food and fragrance of Eden. Like the New Jerusalem, the temple was a microcosm of the perfect harmony of heaven and earth. It is tragic that such a magnificent concept of oneness with God and nature should have been obscured for so long. At a time when we are reaping the bitter harvest of centuries of disrespect for nature, it is important that it should be recovered.

Jesus and the Temple of his Body

It is not hard to see why Jesus, Stephen and Paul were all what might be called 'temple-bashers'. The temple had been built as a paradigm of the whole of creation, but by New Testament times the Jews had obscured this cosmic dimension behind a plethora of ritualism and legalism. They had mistaken the sign for the thing signified. The temple had taken the place of creation as an object of reverence. The trials of Jesus and Stephen, and the arrest of Paul, all centred round their objection to this form of idolatry.

The inner reason for Jesus' hostility to the temple was not just that he was enraged by the corruption of those who "were selling oxen and sheep and pigeons, and the money changers at their business" (*John* 2:14). It was also that, as C.F.D. Moule says, he represented in his own person "the ultimate supersession of the cultus by the reality for which the cultus stands".[25] When the Jews asked him what authority he had for driving the sacrificial animals and the money changers out of the temple courtyard, he said, "Destroy this temple, and in three days I will raise it up". The Jews of course did not understand because, as John explains, "he spoke of the temple of his body" (*John* 2:19,21).

It was this antagonism to the temple as much as his

34

THE TEMPLE AND THE COSMOS

open hostility to the scribes and pharisees which led to his eventual arrest and trial. As John Bowker points out, "the *immediate* issue was concentrated on the extent to which Jesus had repudiated the Temple and, by implication, its authority".[26]

Stephen and the Temple of Creation

The story of the arrest, trial and condemnation of Stephen is meant to be seen as a sequel to the trial and condemnation of Jesus. Like Jesus, Stephen was charged with blasphemy by men who were secretly planted to say: "We have heard him speak blasphemous words against Moses and God" (*Acts* 6:11). As with Jesus, they also set up false witnesses who accused him of speaking against the law and the temple: "This man never ceases to speak words against the holy place and the law; for we have heard him say that this Jesus of Nazareth will destroy this place, and will change the customs which Moses delivered to us" (*Acts* 6:13,14).

Jesus had remained silent before his accusers but Stephen made up for it by delivering the longest sermon recorded in the New Testament apart from the Sermon on the Mount. He did not deny the charges but instead gave the Jewish council a lecture on Abraham, the patriarchs, and Moses. It was a history lesson based on his belief that, just as their forefathers had turned away from Moses, the prophets and the law, they had now in their turn betrayed and murdered Jesus. This was his reply to the accusation that he spoke blasphemously against Moses. As regards the charge that he also spoke against the law, he maintained that the true law was to do with ethics and not animal sacrifices. He quoted Jeremiah and Amos to the effect that justice and righteousness were what the law really required, not burnt offerings and solemn assemblies (*Acts* 7:42-43).

This was also his major contention with regard to the

temple. Just as their forefathers had got along perfectly well without any slain beasts and sacrifices during the forty years in the wilderness, so Abraham, the patriarchs and Moses had all been close to God without needing any temple at all. From Moses to David all they had had was a tent of witness. It was only David who had "asked leave to find a habitation for the God of Jacob" (*Acts* 7:46) which his son Solomon had built.

Stephen was telling the Jews that they had forgotten their history and had made secondary things primary. The faith of Abraham and the patriarchs had come long before the law. The law had come long before the temple. Their priorities were back to front. They needed to be reminded that, at the time of the building of the second temple, Isaiah had affirmed the more ancient and universal truth that God did not live in temples made with hands but rather that he lived in the length, breadth and height of the temple of his creation:

> Yet the Most High does not dwell in houses made with hands; as the prophet says,
> > 'Heaven is my throne,
> > and earth my footstool.
> > What house will you build for me, says the Lord,
> > or what is the place of my rest?
> > Did not my hands make all things?'
> > > > *(Acts* 7:48-50; *Isaiah* 66:1-2)

This particular quotation from Isaiah was Stephen's punch-line. This was the scriptural text which clinched his argument. A significant strand in the prophetic tradition supported this interpretation of Jewish history. Isaiah was only one of many who had said that just as God desired "love not sacrifice" (*Hosea* 6:6) so he also desired to be worshipped in the temple of his creation, not in houses made with hands.[27]

However true this understanding of the law and the prophets might have been, it sounded subversive to those who were committed to the cultus and not to the reality for which the cultus stood. As F.F. Bruce comments, "Real or imagined belittling of the Temple was certain to rouse to fury both the city populace and the priestly party with their vested interests in the building and its cultus."[28] Their reaction was predictable. As they had had little compunction in stoning the prophets and condemning Jesus, so they now made short work of this impudent disciple of the prophet Jesus who put faith, righteousness and the temple of creation before animal sacrifices, solemn assembly and Herod's temple.

Luke, the writer of Acts, obviously saw this sequel to the trial and death of Jesus as definitive of the differences between those who continued to follow the traditional understanding of Moses, the law and the temple, and those who reinterpreted this tradition in the light of Jesus, the new Moses, the law of the heart and the temple of creation. This theme is one of the most important in the Acts of the Apostles, and appears again most noticeably in the preaching and arrest of Paul.

Paul and the Temple not made with Hands

When Paul was on his missionary journeys attempting to convert the people of Athens, he spoke out as strongly against the altars and shrines of Greece as Stephen had done against the Jewish temple. Paul himself was a staunch believer in the concept of a national cultus centred on a sacred shrine (*Acts* 21:26; 24:11) but he was able to extend this concept to embrace a universalism based on God as the creator of all things and all people:

The God who made the world and everything in it, being Lord of heaven and earth, does not live in shrines made by man, nor is he served by human hands, as though he needed anything, since he himself gives to all men life and breath and everything. And he made from one every nation of men to live on all the face of the earth, having determined allotted

37

periods and the boundaries of their habitation, that they should seek God, in the hope that they might feel after him and find him. Yet he is not far from each of us for:

'In him we live and move and have our being'; as even some of your poets have said,

'For we are indeed his offspring.'

(*Acts* 17:24-28)

Stephen had said to his accusers that their historical memory was too short. They had to go farther back into history, to the time before the temple, to see what the law was really about and to the time before the law to see what Abraham's faith was all about. Paul was now encouraging the Greeks to go even farther back than that, to the very beginning of creation when God had made not only everything in heaven and on earth but also all nations and the different countries in which they were to live. In spite of much scholarship which contends that this whole speech reflects a pantheistic view of the deity which is incompatable with the rest of Paul's teaching, I agree with Bertil Gärtner that this universal creationism was at the heart of his gospel for the Gentiles, as distinct from those apostles who remained to some extent bound by nationalistic Judaism. [29] It was also the basis of his belief that Jesus was not just the second Moses, but the second Adam as well.

Like Jesus and Stephen before him, Paul soon found himself in trouble back home for this universalist preaching. When he returned to Jerusalem the following year to tell the apostles about the success of his missionary journeys, only arrest by the Roman guards saved him from summary execution at the hands of the Jewish mob. Their almost uncontrollable violence towards him was based on the same grounds as that which had been shown towards Stephen and Jesus: "This is the man who is teaching men everywhere against the people and the law and this place; moreover he has defiled this holy place" (*Acts* 21:28).

38

It is sobering to reflect that many contemporary Christians, with their pre-occupation with ecclesiastical buildings and lack of serious environmental concern, might have more in common with the Jews who defended the temple than with Jesus, Stephen and Paul. We too seem to be in grave danger of mistaking the sign for the thing signified, the church at the street corner for the church of the universe.

CHAPTER 3

CYCLES OF SEVEN AND THE JEWISH FESTIVALS

So far in this enquiry we have been dealing with the biblical concept of cosmic space as expressed in the models of the New Jerusalem and Solomon's temple. We are now going to attempt to examine aspects of the Old Testament understanding of cosmic time, for only by so doing shall we gain enough background knowledge to see the universal dimension of Christ's ministry in a new light.

Bearing in mind all that we have already established, I believe it is possible to show that the harmony of space built into Solomon's temple found an equivalent embodiment in the Israelites' annual divisions of time. The same principles of number and ratio which we have seen expressed in the spatial proportions of the temple, were also expressed in the times and seasons of their calendrical year. This is most apparent in the timing of the annual festivals which put great emphasis on intervals involving the number seven.

Seven occurs 287 times in the Bible, and is one of the most prevalent numbers in the scriptures. Many well-known instances of its occurrence spring to mind such as Namaan being told to wash seven times in the Jordan; Jesus telling Peter to forgive seventy times seven, and the seven churches in *Revelation*. In fact, there are so many famous instances that, as Maurice Farbridge aptly remarks, "it would indeed be a work of supererogation to go over all the passages of the Bible where it occurs in order to make out that it has a deep significance".[1] Many scholars would go further, agreeing with Ethelbert Bullinger that it "is used as *no other number* is"[2], that it symbolised something holy,[3] sacred,[4] and spiritually perfect.[5]

Yet despite its prevalence and evident importance, at no point do the scriptures tell us explicitly why this should be so. As with so many aspects of the scriptural use of numbers, we have been left to work out this secret for ourselves. Why has the number seven been thought of as holy, sacred and spiritually perfect? What is its deep significance? In attempting to answer these riddles, we shall also lay bare some of the mysteries of cosmic time in the Bible.

The Lunar Quarter

At first glance the answer does not seem hard to find because seven is usually understood to be a lunar number and most scholars would agree with Farbridge that "amongst the Semites the symbolical character of seven originated with the division of the lunar month into quarters".[6] Seven is the nearest whole number to a quarter of the moon's cycle of 29½ days. As we have already discovered "semitic symbolism is based on the belief that there is an analogy between all activities in heaven and everything on earth".[7] It therefore followed that since "the number seven was regarded as sacred in heaven, it must also be held as sacred on earth".[8]

This explanation certainly agrees with much of the biblical record, for the moon was clearly important to the Hebrews and is referred to far more frequently than any other heavenly body except the sun. The new moon is often mentioned together with the sabbath (eg. *2 Kings* 4:23; *Amos* 8:5; *Hosea* 2:13; *Isaiah* 1:13) and was often kept as a feast day. It ranked second only to the sun and was singled out as a special wonder of creation when all the other stars were undifferentiated:

41

When I look at thy heavens, the work of thy fingers,
the moon and the stars which thou hast established;
(Psalm 8:3).

But above all it would appear that the moon was important in Israel because it had been made "to mark the seasons" (Psalm 104:19). It had been appointed as the "lesser light" to rule the night, just as the sun, the "greater light", had been appointed to rule the day. Together with the sun it had been made for "signs and for seasons and for days and years" as the creation story makes clear:

And God said,'Let there be lights in the firmament of the heavens to separate the day from the night; and let them be for signs and for seasons and for days and years, and let them be lights in the firmament of the heavens to give light upon the earth.' And it was so. And God made the two great lights, the greater light to rule the day, and the lesser light to rule the night; he made the stars also.   (*Gen.* 1:14-16)

The central importance of the moon in the measurement of time was basic to the consciousness of early man throughout the world as he began to understand the mysterious workings of the chronometer of the heavens. As J. C. Cooper states "the moon is universally symbolic of the rhythm of cyclic time . . . As periodic re-creation it is Time and measurement, time being first measured by lunar phases".[9]

It was for this reason that seven was used throughout the Bible as a basic unit of time.[10] There were sand and water clocks and a sexagesimal arithmetic to measure the minutes and hours,[11] but the larger units of time were calculated by means of the cycles of the sun and moon. The sun was the clock for the days and years and the moon was the clock for the weeks and months. The two together gave light and regulated the calendar.

The *Genesis* story speaks of the moon being "for signs and for seasons" which in the *N.E.B.* is translated "for festivals and for seasons", in the *Jerusalem Bible* as for "festivals", and in the *T.E.V.* as for "religious festivals". These translations indicate that the Hebrew festivals as well as the weeks and months were regulated by the moon. They also explain why the number seven is so conspicuous in the list of the annual feasts as they are given first in *Exodus*, then in *Numbers* and *Deuteronomy* and finally, in their most comprehensive form, in *Leviticus*.[12] Turning to the latter, it is apparent that the time scheme of the festivals is almost completely made up of cycles of seven.

The Jewish Festivals

In *Leviticus* 23 the first appointed feast was the sabbath of solemn rest "on the seventh day". The second was on the fourteenth (ie. 7 × 2) day of the first month. This was the Passover which was immediately followed on the fifteenth day by the feast of Unleavened Bread which lasted seven days. During these eight days the people remembered their miraculous escape from slavery in Egypt. The next six verses (vv.9-14) speak of the feast of the First Sheaf of the barley harvest which took place on the second day of the feast of Unleavened Bread.[13] Verses 15 to 21 then give the details of the feast of the wheat harvest, the feast of Weeks. This had to be celebrated exactly seven full weeks after the feast of the First Sheaf:

"And you shall count from the morrow after the sabbath, from the day that you brought the sheaf of the wave offering; seven full weeks they shall be, counting fifty days to the morrow after the seventh sabbath; then you shall present a cereal offering of new grain to the Lord" (vv.15-16).

Having enumerated the feasts of the seventh day and the seventh week, the next on the list was the feast of Trumpets which marked the beginning of the seventh month. "In the seventh month, on the first day of the month, you shall observe a day of solemn rest, a memorial proclaimed with blast of trumpets" (v.24). As mentioned above, each new moon was kept as a feast day by the Israelites. The seventh is the only one listed because it was the most important. It was the new moon of the harvest month in a calendar year which began with the spring.[14]

The day of Atonement came next (vv.26-32). This was on the tenth day of the seventh month. It was a day which symbolised at-one-ment or reconciliation, not only with the cycles of seven but also with the law as signified by the tenth day. On this portentous occasion the High Priest entered the Holy of Holies on behalf of the nation, and the people confessed their sins, their "dissonances", and got back in tune with the cosmic harmony of God. N. H. Snaith in his commentary *Leviticus and Numbers* confirms this harmonic and celebratory interpretation when he says:

> Originally this day was a day of great rejoicing, and it was one of the two days in the year when the maidens of Jerusalem went out to dance in the vineyards, apparently a betrothal dance. . . The penitential sorrow of the Day of Atonement is a later development.[15]

The final festival of the year was the feast of Booths or Tabernacles, on the fifteenth day of the seventh month, which lasted seven days (vv.33-36 and 39-43). This was the final harvest-home for the agricultural produce, especially for the fruit, the olive and the grape. It was a joyful time of thanksgiving which ended with prayers for the autumnal rains and the next year's sowing.[16]

This obsession with the rhythm of seven in cyclic time was carried on beyond the feasts which marked the seven days, the seven weeks and the seventh month, into the larger cycles of the years. *Leviticus* 25 lists two more kinds of sabbath which were both based on the rhythm of seven but in these cases the unit of time was not seven days or seven weeks, but seven years and seven weeks of years. The first of these was the seventh or sabbath year, the Sabbatical, which was instituted as a year of rest for all agricultural land:

> The Lord said to Moses 'Say unto the people of Israel, When you come into the land which I give you, the land shall keep a Sabbath to the Lord. Six years you shall sow your field, and six years you shall prune your vineyard, and gather in its fruits; but in the seventh year there shall be a sabbath of solemn rest for the land, a sabbath to the Lord; you shall not sow your field or prune your vineyard.' (vv. 1-4)

The second of these was the fiftieth or Jubilee year which was measured in exactly the same way as the feast of Weeks only in years instead of weeks, but there was also much more to it than that:

> And you shall count seven weeks of years, seven times seven years, so that the time of the seven weeks of years shall be to you forty-nine years. Then you shall send abroad the loud trumpet on the tenth day of the seventh month; on the day of atonement you shall send forth the trumpet throughout all your land. And you shall hallow the fiftieth year, and proclaim liberty throughout the land to all its inhabitants; it shall be a jubilee for you, when each of you shall return to his family. A jubilee shall that fiftieth year be to you; in it you shall neither sow nor reap what grows of itself, nor gather the grapes from the undressed vines. For it shall be a jubilee; it shall be holy to you. (vv. 8-12)

This fiftieth year was the ultimate expression of seven-ness and was very unlike the modern understanding of "jubilee" meaning anniversary. (The only popular expression of its original meaning is probably Henry Clay Work's song *Marching Through Georgia*: "Hurrah! hurrah! we bring the Jubilee! Hurrah! hurrah! the flag that makes you free!", etc.) Firstly, it was a second successive year of rest for the land following on from the Sabbatical of the forty-ninth year.[17] Secondly, it was concerned with the enactment of socio-economic legislation regarding the release of slaves from their terms of service, the cancellation of debts, and the return of property to its original ownership. Thirdly, the Hebrew word *yobel*, from which jubilee is derived, denotes a specific kind of ram's horn which was blown uniquely on that occasion. The Year of Jubilee, *shanat ha yobel*, therefore literally meant the year which was announced by blasts on the horn. In the Hebrew (v. 9) this *yobel* horn blast is described as the *shofar teru'ah*, the *shofar* being the generic word for ram's horn.The difference between the use of the words *yobel* and *shofar* in this context is clarified by Alfred Sendrey in *Music in Ancient Israel* who says that the *yobel* was "the metal sound bell, which could be applied to the *shofar*. It may therefore be assumed with reasonable certainty that the term *yobel* implied an instrument put together of several parts, the most important of which was apparently the sound bell".[18]

17 *The* teru'ah

16 *The* shofar

The Planets and the Great Bear

The Sabbath day, Passover, Unleavened Bread, First Sheaf, Weeks, Trumpets, Atonement, Tabernacles, the Sabbatical and Jubilee year, were thus all festivals which were fitted into a concept of time in which the number seven and its multiples were central. Indeed, the dating of these feasts was so dominated by this number that it almost appears as if the thing that is really being celebrated is the number seven itself, as if it was indeed some sort of sacred entity. Even so it would seem that this obsession with seven had got rather out of hand and that such an overwhelming concentration on a number only associated with the moon's quarter was unwarranted. The "lesser light" might well have been made for the appointment of festivals as well as "for signs and for seasons", but need it have been taken to quite such lengths? Why for instance is it always the moon's quarter that is taken as the basic unit of time? Why not the half or the three quarters, that is, fourteen or twenty-one days? And why are the feast of Weeks and the Jubilee year both reckoned by the computation of seven times seven plus one, when neither forty-nine nor fifty are numbers which relate easily to the moon's cycles? Most pertinent of all, what possible connection can there be between lunar periods and either seven weeks or fifty years? This last question, in particular, prompts the suspicion that the number seven may be so pervasive in the scriptures not only because it is approximately a quarter of the lunar cycle, but also because it had some more profound significance. Once again, although they don't say why, scholars agree that seven times seven was "a specially sacred number".[19] Could it be that despite the foregoing arguments, the number seven was not, after all *primarily* a lunar number?

The fact that the ancient world recognised seven planets could perhaps have been another reason why this number was considered to be so important, but the references to any heavenly body other than the sun and moon are so rare in the Bible that it does not seem likely, in spite of strong arguments to the contrary by some such as Robert Graves in *The White Goddess*[20].

This also applies to the seven stars of the Great Bear which according to scholars, such as Geoffrey Ashe in *The Ancient Wisdom*, was the original source of the sacredness of the heptad.[21] The constellation of Ursa Major in early times was considered to be indestructible because, throughout the year, it never left the northern sky. It appeared to move round the pole and so was associated with the *axis mundi*, the axle of the universe. According to this cosmology, the *axis mundi* gave access to cosmic and divine power so that the temples and holy mountains of many cultures, such as Mount Meru in India, Nippur in Sumer and Safon in Lebanon, were believed to have been built at its base.[22]

There are a few references in the Bible which link Mount Zion with this concept, most notably Psalm 48 where "Mount Zion, in the far north, the city of the great king" appears to be a reference to this universal cosmic mountain. But although God's chariot appeared to Ezekiel "out of the north" (*Ezekiel* 1:4) and Amos spoke of God as "He who made the Pleiades (*A.V.* "the seven stars") and Orion" (*Amos* 5:8) and Jesus Christ had seven stars in his right hand (*Revelation* 1:16), these and a few other indirect references, are not enough on their own to justify such an overt preponderence of the number seven throughout the scriptures. If neither the seven planets nor the seven stars of the Great Bear are enough in themselves to explain this phenomenon, then what other concept is there that would be large enough and universal enough to do so?

Seven Scales and Seven Octaves
There is only one direction in which I believe an answer to this question is likely to be found and that is in the direction of music. Music, as we saw in the last chapter, was known to be the harmonious sounds equivalent to simple numerical ratios. I do not think it is going too far to say that it was this concept of musical harmony which was at the heart of ancient cosmology which was both mirrored in and confirmed by the seven planets and the seven stars of Ursa Major.

As well as being the nearest whole number to a quarter of the moon's cycle, and to a lesser extent the number of the planets and the Great Bear, seven was also known to

48

be the number of notes in the musical scale. This had been discovered on the monochord as early as 3000 B.C. and from it a theory of the harmony of all things had been developed as already indicated.[23] This musical fact, that there were seven notes – not eight or six – corresponded to the celestial fact that there were approximately seven days in the lunar quarter, seven planets and seven stars in the Great Bear. The lunar quarter, the planets and the Great Bear thus all confirmed a theory of music, in which the number seven was seen to be the number of harmony on the earth and in the heavens. According to this theory the number of notes in the musical scale corresponded to the number of days in the week and a complete octave was equivalent to the eight days from sabbath to sabbath.

If the predominance of seven throughout the scriptures and particularly in the timing of the festivals came not primarily from the lunar quarter but from a theory of musical harmony in the microcosm and the macrocosm, it would explain why this number seems to have a life of its own, so universal is its application and symbolism. If it was known as the number of perfection and completion because it was the number of notes in the complete musical scale, then it would automatically coincide with the number associated with the moon's quarter and give to it a much greater importance than it would otherwise have had. This would explain why the obsession with cycles of seven seems to be so predominant in the dating of the festivals, especially those that depended on having to count seven times seven plus one, that is, the feast of Weeks and the Jubilee year. For what possible connection could the numbers 49 and 50 – taken as weeks, or years – have with the lunar cycle?[24] The fact that it was seven times seven that had to be counted, suggests a meaning that might be connected more with seven musical scales than with seven quarters of the moon. If seven times seven plus one was meant to be understood not as a lunar but as a musical number, then the meaning of these numbers becomes obvious because 49 is the number of notes in seven complete scales and 50 is the number in seven full octaves.

Supposing that this musical meaning does explain why seven times seven plus one had to be counted to fix the date of the feast of Weeks and the year of Jubilee, what difference does it make? How does it help to clarify the meaning of the number seven? Are seven octaves musically significant? Only if we can find some profound musical importance in the number 50 will this interpretation seem to be a reasonable one.

The Pythagorean Comma

If we look deeply into harmonic theory, this is precisely what we find. Seven octaves or fifty notes are associated with a mathematical anomaly known as "Pythagoras's Comma" which, like almost everything else attributed to that gentleman, had exercised the minds of mathematicians and musicians for many centuries before he lived. This puzzle consisted in the fact that the measurement of seven octaves and twelve musical fifths, which should have been exactly the same, were found to have a noticeable discrepancy between them.

An octave is measured by doubling the original number which, if taken as 1, gives the number 128 for the seventh octave (ie 1, 2, 4, 8, 16, 32, 64, 128). A fifth is measured by multiples of 1.5 which makes the twelfth fifth come to the number 129.746 (ie 1.5, 2.25, 3.357, 5.062, 7.593, 11.390, 17.086, 25.629, 38.443, 57.665, 86.497, 129.746). Herbert Whone in *The Hidden Face of Music* describes this strange phenomenon which becomes apparent to anyone who is attempting to construct a total key system in perfect fifths. In this case he is starting from the central point of middle C:

> With the central locking point established, the construction of the total key or locking system operates not unpredictably

in series of fives. Moving up from middle C in perfect fifths we arrive at all the sharp keys, G, D, A, E, B, etc., and moving downwards in the same way we arrive at all the flat keys, F, B^b, E^b, A^b, etc. The whole cycle embraces all the twelve half tones of the diatonic scale, and gives a system of scale which . . . . represent all possible type differentiations in a concrete whole.

But in this system there is a strange phenomenon – and it is connected with mathematics. Twelve steps of a perfect fifth in the harmonic system upwards or downwards from middle C, as we have said, brings us back to a C seven octaves (seven signifying completion) distant from it. We can ascertain that the frequency of the upper C is 128 times that of the lower one. But if we take the ratio of the perfect fifth (3:2 or 1.5) we find that our twelve steps increased by a factor of 1.5 bring us to the figure 129.75. The difference is of course known as the comma of Pythagoras. It is a strange phenomenon and a mathematical imponderable in which the octave closes the lock of predictable order and in which the fifth overshooting the mark opens the door to an infinity of frequencies.[25]

If this mathematical and harmonic enigma, known as the "Pythagorean Comma", makes the seventh octave so important, then a musical interpretation of the seven times seven plus one, written into the computation of the feast of Weeks and the Jubilee year, would seem much more likely than a lunar explanation. According to this theory, fifty would be significant because it was related to this Pythagorean musical Comma, not because it was related to the moon's phases. But although this is an intriguing possibility, it raises the deeper question why this Pythagorean Comma was so important that it had to be celebrated in the dating procedure of these two festivals? If this ancient concept of cosmic harmony worked with a theory of correspondences between the earth and the heavens, there would still need to be something equally anomalous in the heavens to justify the conspicuous inclusion of the number 50 in the calendar. The question must therefore be put: what was there in the time-cycles of the heavenly bodies that corresponded to the musical discrepancy between the seventh octave and the twelfth fifth?

Tuning the Moon to the Sun

I believe the answer to this is very straightforward and lies simply in the basic discrepancy between the lunar and the solar year. It was this fundamental celestial anomaly which, in my opinion, corresponded to the musical discrepancy of the Pythagorean Comma. The question we must now ask is, how was this worked out?

Jack Finegan in *Handbook of Biblical Chronology* shows that there were two main influences on the Hebrew's reckoning of the calendar. The first was the Egyptian-Phoenician and the second, the Babylonian. The Egyptian was essentially a solar system and the Babylonian, a luni-solar one. He says that both of these considerably influenced the formation of the Israelite calendar and both used a standardised month of thirty days which was *not* closely related to the moon. In his section "The Israelite Calendar" he says:

It is perhaps not without significance that it is precisely the first two months of the fall and the first two of spring of which the names are preserved in the Old Testament. These are not only times of special importance in Palestinian agriculture but also the times of the two equinoxes. It will also be remembered that in the early period the day was probably reckoned from the morning. These facts suggest that the orientation of this calendar was primarily toward the sun: the rising of the sun began the day; the equinoxes were the turning points of the year. If this was the case then, in the lack of other evidence, the guess may be hazarded that the months were not tied closely to the phases of the moon but were units of the solar year, probably thirty days in length, as in the "schematic" calendars of Egypt and Mesopotamia, and that the resultant shortage of about five days was simply made up by the insertion of additional days at the end of the year.[26]

52

He concludes his argument by saying that "it seems entirely likely that at least from the time of Solomon and under the influence of Egypt and Phoenicia, the calendar of Israel was a schematic solar calendar".[27]

There are many complicating factors regarding the biblical calendar arising from, among other things, the later Babylonian influence, as Finegan goes on to demonstrate; but if we accept this part of his argument, then we may take it that at least from the time of Solomon to the exile, the Hebrews were most probably operating with a calendar of 12 standardised lunar months of 30 days and were not closely adhering to 12 lunar months of 29½ days. Their "lunar" year was thus 360 days (ie. 12 × 30 days) long and not 354 (ie. 12 × 29½). If this were so, then they had approximately 5 extra days to add in to make up the full solar year of 365¼ days.

As far as I can see, it may well have been these 5 extra days which corresponded to the musical discrepancy of the Pythagorean Comma, as a simple piece of arithmetic indicates. If we divide 129.746 (the twelfth fifth) by 128 (the seventh octave), we get 1.0136431. Therefore, 1 to 1.0136431 is the ratio of the two numbers. If we wish to convert this ratio into degrees on a 360 degree circle we must multiply 1.0136431 by 360. This gives 364.91151. If we multiply the difference, ie .0136431 by 360, we get 4.911516. In other words the Pythagorean Comma is equivalent to 4.9 degrees or 4.9 days in the year, thus increasing the total length of the year from 360 to 364.9 days. I find it reasonable to conclude that this "comma" of 4.9 was taken to be equivalent to the 5 extra days which made up an approximation to the full solar year.

In coming to this conclusion I find myself in disagreement with Ernest McClain who in *The Myth of Invariance*, makes the Comma equivalent to 7.2 degrees.[28] I also wonder how Alain Daniélou, in his magisterial work *An Introduction to the Study of Musical Scales*, can say that the correspondence between the

Comma and the sun-moon discrepancy is a *precise* one:

> In reality, the physical laws which are applicable to sound are not particular to them, but are those which regulate all the normal rhythms of the Universe, and those "positive" minds, which smile at such conceptions, might be very embarrassed if Saturday did not come every eighth day, if the days no longer had 24 hours (12 + 12), the hours 60 minutes, and if the relation of the sun and the moon no longer formed for us a cycle of 12 months with, precisely, a slight difference comparable to that of 12 fifths and seven octaves. [29]

I find that I cannot accept what Daniélou appears to be saying without the qualifications that by "12 months" he means 360 not 354 days (ie. standardised, not lunar months), and that by "with, precisely, a slight difference comparable to that of 12 fifths and seven octaves" he does *not* mean that the comparison is exact. I do not see how he can use the word "precisely" when the Comma is equivalent to only 4.9 days and the approximate discrepancy between the lunar and the solar year, even taking it as a schematic 360 days, is 5.25. Even with the Comma there is still a discrepancy of approximately .35 days.

Nevertheless, I believe that the comparison was close enough to be taken as a precise correspondence between heaven and earth, on the "as above, so below" principle and that it was sufficiently exact to be taken to represent the ancient belief that the universe sang and was constructed in accordance with harmony. I believe it was a sufficiently important aspect of the ancient wisdom to be incorporated into the Holiness Code of the Book of the Covenant of *Leviticus*, and that the injunctions to count fifty days to mark the feast of Weeks and fifty years to mark the year of Jubilee can best be explained by means of this cosmology. As Einstein said of one of his theories, it was "too beautiful to be false".

We can now understand why the year of Jubilee was

called the year of the *yobel*, the amplified ram's horn, and why it was announced by repeated blasts on that instrument. For this was the year which celebrated the completion of the cycle of seven "octave-years". It also celebrated the completion of the cycle of twelve "fifth-years" and the discrepancy between the two.

This fundamental musical anomaly also had deep theological meaning in the ancient world, for it was evidently seen as a metaphor for both the discord of man's sinfulness and also of the hope of his ultimate resurrection. David Tame in *The Secret Power of Music* has an appendix on "The Mystery of Pythagoras' Comma" in which he clearly defines these two profound spiritual interpretations of the Comma. First he speaks about it as a symbol of man's fallenness:

> The comma produces huge cosmological, as well as practical, implications and results. Since this system of calculating twelve notes (ie. by perfect fifths) does not perfectly complete the octave, the specific twelve pitches it produces are imperfect for use together in harmony. They do not perfectly harmonise since they do not divide the octave into perfectly accurate divisions of twelve as, say, the hours of a clock do perfectly divide a clock face. Yet to adjust their slight pitch discrepancies in order to produce perfect harmony would render each note imperfect as an interval of a fifth, or as a ratio of 3:2. The perfecting of their musical system was paramount to the ancients, for their music had to harmonize with the eternal laws of the universe. Therefore the perfect ratio of 3:2 and its interval of a perfect fifth were regarded as sacred and inviolable. If the system resulted, as it did, in the harmony of mortal music being imperfect, then this had to be borne as a manifest symbol of man's fall from grace, and of the inherent imperfection of the non-heavenly realm of time and space.[30]

He then goes on to speak of the other, complementary spiritual significance of the Comma, that of the hope of ultimate resurrection:

Though the comma may be a symbol of the imperfection of man's mortal state, the very same comma simultaneously provides the way back to the original state of perfection. For the comma is not a slight interval *less* than seven octaves, but *in excess* of them. In the ancient world, this fact was widely conceived as a symbol of *renewal*. The cycle of twelve perfect fifths did not *close* and finish a cycle of seven octaves, but exceeded it, and thus, as it were, spiralled *upward*. There is evidence that this upward spiral of renewal was mystically associated with the widespread ancient myth of the phoenix, the archetypal "bird" which is resurrected from its own ashes. Pythagoras' comma, then, can be seen as God's own engram written into the very law of the universe and of physics. And it is by the nature of this engram that man is heir to the promise of eventual resurrection and ascension out of the dim caverns of mortality.[31]

Such passages demonstrate convincingly why the Comma was considered to be so spiritually, as well as musically and cosmically, important. Tame impressively confirms my belief that the Israelite calendar embodies this spirituality in its computation of the feast of Weeks and the Jubilee year. This is particularly so with regard to the latter, the *shanat ha yobel*, the year of the *yobel*. The fact that the Jubilee year was announced by repeated blasts on the *yobel* on the day of Atonement indicates a close correspondence with "Pythagorean" cosmology. For this year of release was proclaimed on the most sacred of Jewish musical instruments by a series of repeated blasts on the *fundamental* and *fifth* notes! It was quite literally the musical expression of all that the ancient world believed about their spirituality and its relation to cosmic harmony.

The "Octave" Year of Twelve "Semi-tone" Months

This basic correspondence between the music of the earth and the music of the heavens indicates that the positioning of the seven major Jewish festivals in the spring, early summer and autumn was most probably based not only on the seasons of the agricultural year and the equinoxes, but also on a musical division of the calendar in which each month represented the semitone of an octave. This is certainly the contention of David Tame:

> It was believed that the twelve Tones really did express themselves individually to a greater degree according to the month of the year, the time of day, and so forth. A particular Tone "sounded" more prominently in a particular month, and during a particular hour of the day.[32]

If this was indeed the case in Israel then Passover, Unleavened Bread and First Sheaf would, in the first month, be equivalent to the first tone, that is, the fundamental or tonic; the feast of Weeks, or Pentecost, as it was later called, in the third month, would be equivalent to a minor third, and Trumpets, Atonement and Tabernacles, in the seventh month, would be equivalent

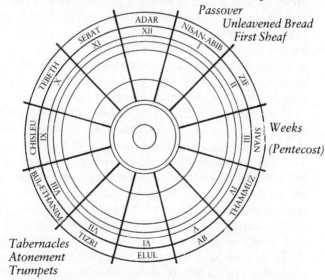

18 The festivals as the minor triad

to the seventh semitone counting from the tonic, that is, the fifth, the dominant interval. Is it more than coincidence that these three notes form the minor triad? Could this be the origin of the frequent recurrence of the minor triad in Israeli folk music to this day?

It might also be possible on this analysis to speculate that the feast of Trumpets was held on the first day of the seventh month, not only because it marked the beginning of the harvest month and the ecclesiastical New Year, but also because it celebrated the month of the seventh semitone, the fifth - the very note which was the dominant interval of the trumpets themselves! By the same analogy, the year of Jubilee would be ushered in on the tenth day of the seventh month not only because it was Old New Year's Day,[33] but also because that day symbolised the coming together of the number 7 representing harmony and the number 10 representing the law. The proclamation of freedom for the slaves and the ending of leaseholds on property would be the social expression of this harmonious law. The blasts on the ram's horn would be blown to celebrate the dominant harmonic, as on the feast of Trumpets, but this time the metal sound bell would have been added which turned the *shofar* into the *yobel* and greatly amplified the instrument's sound, as befitted the greater occasion.

The tenth day of the seventh month of the fiftieth year, was thus the moment of supreme at-one-ment with the rhythms and cycles of God as expressed in his cosmos. The day of Atonement which ushered in the year of Jubilee symbolised *par excellence* the tuning of all things on earth to the harmony of all things in heaven. It epitomised an obsession with harmony which is evident throughout all the feasts and festivals of the Levitical year, and in the incidence of the number 7 throughout the Bible. It was because of its centrality to this harmonic cosmology that I believe the number 7 came to be thought of as holy, sacred and spiritually perfect.

This comprehensive concept of harmony was intended to be put into practice throughout the whole of life and to bring about harmonious relationships between God, his people and his creation. All the feasts and festivals were understood to be the "fortes" of rhythms which were supposed to be resonating concordantly throughout the land all the time. The temple had been built to express these rhythms in space. The festivals were appointed to express them in time. The whole of the law was thus designed to express them in the continuum of space-time, so that all people and all things should always be in tune, in time, and in phase with each other, nature and God.

We shall see how this interpretation of the Jewish festivals, particularly with regard to Weeks or Pentecost and Jubilee, will help us rediscover the cosmic dimension in the ministry of Jesus Christ.

CHAPTER 4

THE PULSE OF THE UNIVERSE

Having threaded our way through some of the complexities of Old Testament time-cycles and arrived at what is, I hope, a reasonable hypothesis regarding the cosmology behind the Israelite calendar, it is time to capitalise on our findings. Now that we have learnt something about the background, we can begin to look at the ministry of Jesus, particularly at what is usually known as "The Mission of the Seventy" (*Luke* 10:1-24).

In the last chapter the two most difficult questions we raised about the Hebrew calendar were: why did *Leviticus* command that 7 full weeks or 50 days be counted from the feast of the First Sheaf, in order to compute the correct day for the celebration of the feast of Weeks (*Lev.* 23:15,16); and why was the same procedure enjoined, counting not days but weeks of years in order to observe the correct year for the Jubilee (*Lev.* 25:8-12)? The answer we arrived at was that the 7 × 7 + 1 that had to be counted on both these occasions could not be completely explained by assuming that biblical scholars had been right when they had traditionally associated the number 7 primarily with an approximation to a quarter of the moon's monthly cycle of 29½ days. Rather, we came to the conclusion that the number 7 referred in the first instance to the musical scale of seven major tones and that the numbers 49 and 50 referred to seven scales and seven octaves respectively.

We then went on to explain the theory of the Pythagorean Comma and its approximate correspondence with the differential between the lunar and the solar year. We assumed that the Israelite calendar was strongly influenced in pre-exilic times by the Mesopotamian, Egyptian and Phoenician calendars which were basically solar and had 12 schematic months of 30 days, making up a 360 day year. We calculated that the Pythagorean Comma of ratio 129.746 to 128 was equivalent to 4.9 degrees and that these 4.9 degrees did duty for the 5 extra days which made up the full solar year of 365, to the nearest day. We realised that this was not a precise equivalence because it still fell short of the actual solar year of 365¼ days by approximately .35 of a day, but nevertheless we held that it was *taken* to be so by the ancients in their theory of cosmic harmony – "as above, so below".

The Mission of the Seventy or Seventy-Two

We have assumed that the 4.9 degrees of the Pythagorean Comma was taken to be equivalent to the 5 extra days that made up the full solar year. If we reckon therefore that the 4.9 was equivalent to these 5 days, then we may also assume that these 5 days were 1/72 of the year, since 360 divided by 5 = 72. The ratio of the Pythagorean Comma to the year may thus be taken as 1 to 72.

If you read the *New English Bible* you will notice that in *Luke* 10 verses 1 and 17 the number 72 is mentioned: "After this the Lord appointed a further seventy-two and sent them on ahead of him in pairs . . ." etc, and "The seventy-two came back jubilant . . ." etc. You may never have had this small detail drawn to your attention before, especially if you have been used to the *A.V.* and the *R.S.V.*, for both of these translations use the number 70 and not 72 and hence have given rise to the traditional title of this passage "The Mission of the Seventy". In the footnote of the *R.S.V.* it says "Other ancient authorities read *seventy-two*", and the footnote in the *N.E.B.* says "Some witnesses read *seventy*". From other recent translations such as the *Jerusalem Bible*, *Good News for Modern Man* and the *New International Version* it is clear that 72 has now become the more acceptable rendering. Why should this be so? Why should most modern versions opt for 72 rather than 70? Does that mean that 72 is the more authentic? There is a deeper question, which is: why should Jesus have a mission of the seventy or seventy-two at all? Wasn't the mission of the 12 apostles enough? Why either 70 or 72?

Turning to a number of commentaries I found that some saw no particular significance in either number,[1] but most thought that the number 70 traditionally represented all the nations of the world (as in *Genesis* 10), and that Jesus was symbolically inaugurating his mission to the Gentile world.[2] Some of these also thought that Jesus, as the second Moses, needed to have 70 elders to share his Spirit and ministry, just as the first Moses had before him.[3] The analogy between this and the ministry of our present-day churches would be that the 12 apostles were like the Roman Catholics and the Anglo-Catholics, while the 70 elders were all like good free churchmen, the former representing the hierarchy and the latter the ordinary working chaps! Be that as it may, I noticed that commentators varied considerably regarding the use of the number 70 or 72. For instance E. Earle Ellis, although he admitted that he didn't know for certain which number was the more authentic, went on to stress the importance of the number which he assumed was 70 not 72:

The number had a weighty pedigree in Old Testament and late Jewish tradition. There were seventy Gentile nations (Gen 10), seventy Israelites going into Egypt as the seed of the future people of God (Exod 1:5), seventy elders who accompanied Moses upon the holy mount and who received a portion of his prophetic spirit (Exod 24:1; Num 11:25). A similar number (plus the high priest) composed the Sanhedrin, the ruling representatives of the nation Israel. It is highly probable that in the present context the number is symbolic and theologically significant.[4]

Unfortunately he did not go on to speculate as to what that symbolic and theological significance might have been. G. H. P. Thompson was equally undecided except that he included two extra elders, Eldad and Medad, who do in fact bring the number of the free churchmen up to 72: "Seventy, or 'seventy-two' (*R.S.V.* margin; the MSS evidence is divided) could be reminiscent of the seventy or seventy-two (if Eldad and Medad are included) elders who were appointed to assist Moses in the leadership of Israel (*Num* 11:10-30)".[5]

In an earlier commentary by John Martin Creed, I found a very interesting observation which suggested that 72 might have been the more authentic number. He argues that "There would be a tendency to make 72 into a round number. Similar confusion between 70 and 72 occurs in Gen X, (the numbers of the peoples) as between [the Hebrew and the Septuagint]; likewise in the traditional number of the Greek translators of the O.T."[6] This last reference, to the Septuagint, we shall come to in a moment. His belief that "there would be a tendency to make 72 into a round number" rang a bell with me because I could imagine that 70 might well have become shorthand for 72, just as I believe "ten cubits from brim to brim" (ie. the diameter) and "thirty cubits measured its circumference" (*1 Kings* 7:23) was shorthand for π (*pi*: 22/7) times 10, ie 31.4159 in the measurements of the brazen sea, the bronze urn outside Solomon's temple. Another commentator, E. J. Tinsley, strengthened me in the conviction of this likelihood. Tinsley appears to have little doubt about 72 being the original reading:

Seventy-two is the number given in the Greek translation of the Hebrew Old Testament, the Septuagint, for the nations of the world in Genesis 10, and Numbers 11:24,26 seems to indicate seventy-two as the number of Moses' elders. Most probably this is the original reading, and 'seventy' crept in later because of its more common use as a symbol for something universal [7]

According to Tinsley "seventy crept in later because of its more common use as a symbol for something universal". I can just see 70 creeping in stealthily and pushing out poor old 72!

Finally, in an attempt to settle this point, I consulted Bruce Metzger's summary of all the primary sources of these texts, but noted his inconclusive opinion that "the number of Jesus' disciples referred to in Luke 10 cannot be determined with confidence".[8] However, in *A Textual Commentary on the Greek New Testament*, where he repeats his belief that the "two" of seventy-two should only be printed in brackets, I observed that Kurt Aland disagreed. The substance of his disagreement is that 72 appears in so few texts compared with 70 that "it is astonishing that the reading *ebdomekonta duo* occurs at all in 10.1 and 17, and that it has such strong support". Such strong support he says, would normally be taken to mean that it was the original reading. He then amplifies Creed and Tinsley's point about the rounding down of 72 to 70:

If in addition the opposing reading lies under the suspicion of ecclesiastical "normalizing", the testimony becomes irrefutable. The opposing witnesses represent entirely an ecclesiastical normalizing. That they are in the majority is altogether understandable; if they are ancient, this only proves how early the normalizing process began to operate. For these reasons *ebdomekonta duo* should be printed without square brackets.[9]

I find this conclusion much more satisfactory than Metzger's and so does Howard Marshall who, with commendable brevity says "the use of 72 is much less frequent. Hence intrinsic probability strongly favours 72".[10]

We may therefore take it that there are good grounds for believing that 70 has done duty for the original number 72. This would confirm the legend that the Septuagint, which in Latin is short for *interpretatio septuaginta seniorum* (ie. the "translation of the seventy elders'), was in fact the translation of the *seventy-two* elders. As the *Encyclopaedia Judaica* states:

The Greek version of the Bible known as the Septuagint . . . probably owes its name to a story related in the *Letter of Aristeas*, according to which 72 scholars, summoned from Jerusalem by Ptolemy II, Philadelphus (3rd C.B.C.), achieved a perfect Greek translation of the Pentateuch, which was deposited in the Alexandrian library. This story was embellished with time until the 72 interpreters were credited with the translation of the entire Hebrew Bible. It was maintained that although each of them had worked independently, their finished versions were identical and moreover, superior to the original as a result of divine inspiration.[11]

Other accounts add that the whole of the translation of the 72 scholars was completed in 72 days.

I wonder if I am beginning to labour the point? Perhaps; but obviously, if it is one which has been in doubt for so long and is central to my argument, then it is worth spending time attempting to settle it. However, I am now satisfied that I have adduced enough evidence to show that where the number 70 has been used in *Luke* 10 and possibly in other parts of the Bible, it is probably referring to the number 72. This is very important because if, as E. J. Tinsley indicates, these numbers were symbols "for something universal", we are more likely to be able to hazard a guess as to what that universal "something" was if, for 70, we can now legitimately read 72.

Why did the number 72 symbolise "something universal" and what was that universal something? Why did Jesus appoint "a further seventy-two"? Why did the seventy-two come back jubilant? Why not 69, 75 or 80? Why was it that it was specifically the number 72?

Just as our theory of the Pythagorean Comma in relation to the Hebrew calendar seems to have much more going for it the deeper we look into it, so this same Comma might provide the key to unlock the secrets of the number 72. Is the ratio of the 5 days to the 360-day year, ie.1 to 72, which we established was the approximate ratio of the Comma to the annual cycle, in some way connected with the universal something which the number 72 symbolises in the Bible? Is it more than a coicidence that this Comma ratio as we have defined it is 1 to 72?

One Day in the Great Year

It could very well be more than a coincidence that 72 appears so prominently in the Comma ratio because, if the Comma represents 5 days in the year, then it would take 72 years to make up a complete year of Commas. 72 years would thus be equivalent to 1 year of Pythagorean Commas. Now, as it happens, 72 years is a very significant unit of time because it is one degree or one "day" of what is known variously as the "Great Year", the "Platonic Year", or the "Cosmic Year."

Without going into too much detail, the Great, Platonic, or Cosmic Year is measured by the time it takes for what is called "the precession of the equinoxes" to complete a cycle. This precession is defined in *Everyman's Encyclopaedia* as "A westward movement of the equinoxes on the ecliptic so that they advance to meet the stars and the sun on its annual return". Its discovery is usually credited to Hipparchus (c 160 – 120 BC.) but, as with many so-called "Pythagorean" discoveries, it was probably known many centuries earlier.[12] It is caused by "the pull of the sun and moon, the moon in particular, on the equatorial bulge of the earth. The tendency of the pull is to make the equator coincide with the ecliptic, but the spinning of the earth prevents this and the phenomenon of Precession takes place".[13] We have spoken about the *axis mundi*, the axle of the world round which the universe was believed to spin. We must now imagine that axis wobbling like a top or an old cartwheel. Giorgio de Santillana and Hertha von Dechend speak about this less well-known dimension of the earth's movement in *Hamlet's Mill*, their great essay on myth and the frame of time:

Its cause is a bad habit of the axis of our globe, which turns around in the manner of a spinning top, its tip being in the centre of our small earth-ball, whence our earth axis, prolonged to the celestial North Pole, describes a circle around the North Pole of the ecliptic, the time "centre" of the planetary system, the radius of this circle being of the same magnitude as the obliquity of the ecliptic with respect to the equator: 23½. The time which this prolonged axis needs to circumscribe the ecliptical North Pole is roughly 26,000 years, during which period it points to one star after another : around 3,000 B.C. the Pole Star was alpha Draconis; at the time of the Greeks it was beta Ursa Minoris; for the time being it is alpha Ursa Minoris ; in A.D. 14,000 it

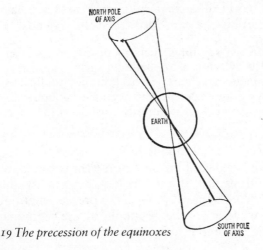

19 The precession of the equinoxes

will be Vega. The equinoxes, the points of intersection of ecliptic and equator, swinging from the spinning axis of the earth, move with the same speed of 26000 years along with the ecliptic. The Sun's position among the constellations at the vernal equinox was the pointer that indicated the "hours" of the precessional cycle – very long hours indeed, the equinoxial sun occupying each zodiacal constellation for about 2200 years.[14]

These details about the astronomy of the Great Year are very complicated for those who know little about this science. It is sufficient for us to be aware in outline of what it is and also how long it takes. It is usually computed, as Santillana and Dechend state, at around 26,000 years; but authorities vary as to its precise length. One gives it as 25,765[15] another as 25,816,[16] another as 25,827[17] and yet another as 25,920. It might seem arbitrary for me to say that I favour the last of these, but I have as good a reason for doing so as for preferring 72 to 70 in the earlier discussion. I believe that whatever the precise astronomical length the Great Year was believed to be, it was *taken* as 25,920 years for the sake of the musical cosmology which, as we have seen, dominated the thought world of ancient cultures. Ernest McClain explains this in his chapter "Music and the Calendar":

> About all we can say for certain about the precessional number 25920 (which is astronomically slightly too large, according to modern measures) is that it fits beautifully into the cosmology of those people who never tried to break the original bonds between music, mathematics and astronomy.[18]

All that McClain says about 25,920 in relation to the exact astronomical length of the Great Year is similar to what we said earlier about the 4.9 degrees of the Pythagorean Comma in relation to the precise length of the solar year. It is another example of the harmonic number being *taken* to be equivalent to the astronomical one. Elsewhere in his chapter, McClain shows how 25,920 is related to ancient Eastern music and cosmology associated with the *Rig Veda*. Alain Daniélou also makes this connection in terms which recall Carl Sagan's discussion about Hindu time-cycles in relation to modern theories about the duration of the universe:

> The Pythagorean great year is the fifth part of the Chinese great year of Yuan, equal to $25,920 \times 5 = 129,600$, itself the double of the Hindu manvantara, $25,920 \times 2\frac{1}{2} = 64800$ which, according to Eastern doctrine, always brings humanity back to its starting point. The duration of this complete evolution being two and a half precessions.[19]

It is on the basis of this ancient and apparently universal musical cosmology, as explained by McClain and Daniélou, that I believe we can claim the Great Year was held to be 25,920 years long. If we divide this number by 12 we get a "month" of 2,160 years and if we divide this month by 30 we get a "day" of 72 years. This unit of 72 years is thus one "day" in the Great Year. I suggest that we may have arrived at last at a reasonable explanation as to why the number 72 and the ecclesiastically normalised number of 70 should signify "something universal" in the Bible. It is possible to go even further and say that this unit of 72 years was one "day" in the Cosmic Year because it represented one complete cycle of Pythagorean Commas. We must remember that David Tame speaks in the most far-reaching terms about the Comma's significance:

> The comma is a strange and wide-ranging phenomenon, being literally 'written into' the physical and mathematical laws of the universe. We are entering here into regions of thought difficult for the Western mind to grasp, but the possibility seems to be that it is by the phenomenon of Pythagoras' Comma that the very nature of our lives within the realm of mortality is arranged.[20]

Tame here makes enormous claims for the importance of the Comma and seems to suggest that it may be connected in some way to the very pulse of creation.

Rachaph and the Primal Vibration

Tame speaks at length elsewhere about the physics of vibration and indeed constantly returns to the fundamental link between music, vibration and the created universe. In the section called "Primal Vibration" he enlarges on his basic contention that the ancients throughout the world believed that "this Cosmic Vibration was the origin and basis of all matter and energy in the Universe".[21] In a characteristically arresting paragraph, he links this ancient wisdom with modern science and with various religious traditions:

> And thus we find ourselves throwing light upon the widely-held belief that all matter is composed of one basic substance or energy. According to the great thinkers of old, this energy was Vibration. In modern times, the physical sciences are now arriving back at this original point of departure. Once again, science is beginning to suspect that matter is all composed of one fundamental something, and that the frequencies or rhythms of this something determine the specific nature of each object and atom.
>
> The universal vibratory energies were called by the ancient Egyptians the Word of Words of their Gods; to the Pythagoreans of Greece they were the Music of the Spheres; and the ancient Chinese knew them to be the celestial energies of perfect harmony. The Cosmic Tones, as differentiations of the OM, were the most powerful force in the universe according to the ancients, for these Tones *were* the universe – the very source of the Creation itself.[22]

Vastly impressive though this is, I confess I was surprised that the Egyptians, the Pythagoreans, the Chinese and the Hindus evidently knew all about this primal vibratory force, but not the Hebrews. Although Tame speaks in another chapter, about the biblical concept of the Logos, the Word, I was puzzled that his specific references to *vibration* did not include the Bible. Did its writers not know about it? Did they not even have a word for the basic pulsing energy of the universe?

There is a word in Hebrew which, among other things, can be construed as meaning "to vibrate". It is referred to by Gerhard von Rad, a leading Old Testament scholar, in his commentary on *Genesis* at 1:2: "and the Spirit of God was moving over the face of the waters". The word *merachepet* is usually translated "moved" or "hovered", which he says can also be rendered "vibrate":

> The much-disputed *merachepet* (L:*schwebte*, "hovered") is not to be translated by "brood", but according to Deut 32:11 and Jer 23:9, the verb appears to have the meaning of "vibrate", "tremble", "move", "stir". This is supported by Dan 7:2, which is to be referred to for interpretation.[23]

This I found most encouraging and was even more surprised to find that another commentator, from a different theological background, went even further than von Rad in this vibratory interpretation. In *Exposition of Genesis*, H.C.Leupold says "The verb *rachaph* from which the piel participle is used, *mera(ch)chepheth*, signifies a vibrant moving, a protective hovering".[24] Answering the question, what was the purpose of the Spirit moving over the face of the waters? he goes on to say:

> We could never believe that this hovering of the Spirit over the face of the waters was idle and purposeless. From all other activities that are elsewhere ascribed to the Holy Spirit we conclude that His work in this case must have been anticipatory of the creative work that followed, a kind of impregnation with divine potentialities. The germs of all that is created were placed into dead matter by Him. His was the preparatory work for leading over from the inorganic to the organic. Koenig in his *Kommentor* feels impelled to interpret

this "hovering" as "an intensified and vitalised type of vibration". We should not be averse to holding that the foundation for all physical laws operative in the world now was laid by this preparatory activity.[25]

If we follow von Rad and Leupold, we are justified in asserting that the Hebrews did have their own word for vibration from the root *rachaph* and that they too can take their place in Tame's list of ancient cultures who knew about the creative power of the primal vibration. In passing it is worth mentioning how strange it is that Tame has not seen how very similar *Genesis* 1:2 is to his description of the descent of the Word, as a vibratory force, on the waters of creation. He refers to the Egyptian creation story but could just as well have been decribing the biblical "Spirit of God *vibrating* over the face of the waters", when he says:

Only two force principles are at work in everything: matter and dynamic energy. Here, 'matter' equates with the primeval Celestial Waters of the ancient Egyptians. By 'dynamic force' is meant God manifest; meaning the descent of the Word into the Celestial Waters. The descent of this vibratory force gives rise, at its different frequency-levels, to all the supposedly different forms of energy.[26]

This passage reads like a further development of the interpretations of von Rad and Leupold, as if Tame was, like them, a biblical scholar. The likeness is quite remarkable. But what is even more remarkable, and apparently confirmatory of Tame's inadvertent exposition of *Genesis* 1:2, is the numerical significance of the Hebrew root word *rachaph*. If we analyse the gematria of the three root letters according to the letter-number equivalents as mentioned in chapter 3, we get r = 200, ch = 8 and ph = 80, so that the total is 288. This number, according to Rabbinic tradition of Chassidic Judaism, represented the 288 sparks into which the Spirit of God divided at the moment of creation on its way into substantiality,[27] but even more significantly for our present study, it will be noticed that 288 is 4 × 72. It is also in an octave relationship to 72 because, as demonstrated in the last chapter, octave levels go up and down in multiples and divisions of 2. Thus the octave levels from 288 downwards would be 144, 72, 36, 18, 9, etc. This in itself indicates that if we are meant to read a musical significance into the numerology of the word "vibrate", then 72 is in harmonic relation to the pulse of creation. The Pythagorean Comma and one "day" in the Great Year is thus also written into the Bible as well as into "the physical and mathematical laws of the universe", as Tame contends.

The Singers and Trumpeters in the Temple

In *The Myth of Invariance*, it is striking to notice how frequently Ernest McClain refers to the numbers 288 and 72 as octave levels in his section "Postscript on the Creation of the World".[28] He analyses the singing in Solomon's temple according to a double octave in which the terminal indices are 288 and 120. These numbers he gets from *1 Chronicles* 25:7-8 where, as we discovered in chapter 3, the number of Levites "who were trained in singing to the Lord, all who were skilful, was two hundred and eighty-eight" and from *2 Chronicles* 5:12 where, as we also found, there were "a hundred and twenty priests who were trumpeters". The details of how he works out the notation of this double octave need not concern us except that the octave levels themselves are 288, 144, and 72, with the 288 to 144 being the lower octave. It is perhaps significant that if we imagine that the two rooms of the temple of Solomon represented two octaves, with the lower octave being the Holy Place and the higher octave, the Holy of Holies, then 288 would be the fundamental note at the entrance wall of the Holy Place and 144 would be the octave higher at the wooden screen which divided the two chambers. The number 72 would then be the double octave note at the far end wall of the Holy of Holies. These vibrating tones, the primal vibrations that were entoned at the dedication of the temple, may have been the same as those which vibrated in the beginning over the face of the deep. That is to say, the consonances of the universe which, we observed, were built into the proportions of the temple may have been the same as those associated with the Spirit moving, vibrating, ie. "288-ing" over the waters at the dawn of creation. If this was so then the 288, 144, 72 double octave might well have been the Hebrew expression of the universal OM, or Cosmic Sound.[29] These may well have been the numbers which represented the overtones of the pulse of the universe.

Holy of Holies   20 The two octaves of the Temple

We saw in chapter 3 that something very strange happened at the dedication of the temple when the 288 singers and 120 trumpeters raised the song in unison and the whole place was filled with a cloud. We established then that this could be explained by the vibrations of the perfect harmony expressed in the microcosm calling forth the Divine response from the macrocosm. We can now go further and propose that this perfect harmony was vibrating on the overtones of *rachaph*, the Hebrew word for the primal creative sound, associated with the double octave 288, 144 and 72.

This may also give us a new interpretation of the mysterious measurement of the wall of New Jerusalem, where St John says "He also measured its wall, a hundred and forty-four cubits by a man's measure, that is, an angel's" (*Rev.* 21:17). If this 144 was meant to be understood as an octave level, then it would be equivalent to the wall of partition between the Holy of Holies and the Holy Place and, like 72, would be harmonically related to 288, the primal pulse of creation. This should not surprise us because the New Jerusalem was, as we have seen, an expanded version of the Holy of Holies. It was the cosmic cube which contained all the consonances – the primal vibrations – of the universe.

Harmonic 288

In connection with these harmonic numbers of primal vibration, I have been trying to assess a book written by Bruce Cathie. On the flyleaf it says of him:

He probes into space-time, throws new light on Einstein's famous $E = MC^2$, and discusses the harmonics of light, sound, temperature, lasers, plant growth and human health. He also shows how scientists, when ready to break out of their present narrow disciplines into the immeasurably wide fields he has thrown open to them, will be able to carry human knowledge to heights undreamed of including life on other planets ... Far-fetched? Too fantastic? The most sceptical reader cannot fail to be impressed by Bruce Cathie's cool and methodical presentation of the facts, and to agree that the harmonic of the speed of light is the key to the understanding of all life and all matter, and to the mysteries of the universe itself.[30]

Isn't that truly amazing! What did I find was the number of the speed of light according to Bruce Cathie? Why, nothing less than our old friend 144, of course – and without any biblical help! And what is the title of this book? Why, *The Pulse of the Universe*, of course. And what is its sub-title? *Harmonic 288* – it had to be didn't it? Does Bruce Cathie confirm from his knowledge of the new physics, all that we have deduced from our study of biblical cosmology? Are 72, 144 and 288 related to the pulse beat of the modern, as well as the ancient understanding of the universe? Is it, after all, "by the phenomenon of Pythagoras' Comma that the very nature of our lives within the realm of mortality is arranged"?[31] *The Hitch-hiker's Guide to the Galaxy* must be wrong! The answer "to the Ultimate Question of Life, the Universe and Everything"[32] is *not* forty-two as Deep Thought proclaimed, but seventy-two. "After this the Lord appointed a further seventy-two" – to keep the pulse of his universe.

Is it only a coincidence that the pulse beat of the average adult in good health is 72 per minute? And is it, further, a coincidence that the numbers of the penatagon-pentagram are 5 and 72? Perhaps David and Solomon were even wiser than we have so far discovered when they planned and built the pentagonal door into the Holy of Holies, for the numbers 5 and 72 link man with the universe.[33]

CHAPTER 5

GREAT NEW YEAR'S DAY

In the last chapter we established that the most likely meaning of the symbolic number 72 in the Bible as a whole and particularly in Jesus' "Mission of the Seventy Two", was that it was a cosmic number and that as a number of years, it was one "day" in the Great Year of 25,920 years.

The question I would now like to ask is, are these two references to this number the only indications that New Testament writers were aware that there was such a thing as the Great Year? Not many of us today know of its existence. Could it be that they were so knowledgeable, where we are so ignorant? Did they really know what the time was on this cosmic clock of the precession of the equinoxes? If you had said to one of them "What's the cosmic time, please?" would he have known what you were talking about? In an attempt to answer this, we turn to the New Testament to see if there was any consensus about the times they were living in. Was there any overall consciousness that these were good times, bad times, special or unique times? Was there a general mood, a spirit of the times, an attitude towards their age, epoch or period in history and if so how was it defined?

Not the End of the World but the End of the Age

These questions are not hard to answer. Yes, there definitely was a prevalent attitude to the times they were living in. They were times which were generally thought of as "the last days" as many well-known texts demonstrate. For instance, the writer to the Hebrews begins "In many and various ways God spoke of old to our fathers by the prophets; but *in these last days* he has spoken to us by a Son". Sometimes the figure of speech changes from the last days to the last hour as in *1 John* 2:18 "Children, it is *the last hour*; and as you have heard that antichrist is coming, so now many antichrists have come; therefore we know that it is *the last hour*". These metaphors, which feature the Greek word *eschatos* meaning "last", sometimes change to "the last times". Speaking of Christ it says in *1 Peter* 1:20 "He was destined before the foundation of the world but was made manifest *in the last of the times (ep'eschatou tōn chronōn)* for your sake". Although the word for "times" here is *chronos*, the *Jerusalem Bible* translates it "ages", saying Christ "has been revealed only in our time, the end of the ages".

This free rendering of *chronos* as "ages", leads on to other well-known texts associated with the New Testament consciousness of living at the *end* of an epoch. These are those which are connected with the actual word for "ages", *aiōnōn*. This word, from which we get our word "aeons", is often translated as "world" in the *A.V.* so that, for instance, the traditional reading of *1 Corinthians* 10:11 is "and they are written for our admonition, upon whom *the ends of the world* are come". The *R.S.V.*, which aims at closer adherence to the Greek, corrects this to "upon whom *the end of the ages* has come". This *A.V.* translation of *aiōn* as "world" has been equally misleading in *Hebrews* 9:26 where it says of Christ "but now once in the end of the world hath he appeared to put away sin by the sacrifice of himself". Once more the word is *aiōnōn*, (not *cosmos*:world), a genitive plural, which should read "he has appeared once for all at the *end of the ages*". The *R.S.V.* and the *Jerusalem Bible* are also not strictly accurate here, putting "age" in the singular. The *N.E.B.* is too free, speaking about "at the climax of history". The *Good News Bible* is the most accurate with "when all ages of time are nearing their end".

This translation of *aiōnōn* as "world" when it should mean "ages", has led to the traditional belief that the New Testament writers thought that they were living through not just the end of an age but the end of the *world*. This, together with the frequent rendering of the singular *aiōn*, age also as "world", as, for example, in *Matthew* 28:20 "And, lo, I am with you alway, even unto the end of the world", has obscured the fact that in certain texts some of the New Testament writers appear to have been conscious that they were living through a period they characterised not only as "the last days", but also, as "the end of the ages". I believe that this confusion over the different translations of the words *aiōn* and *aiōnōn* may have stopped us seeing a possible link between their consciousness of the times in general and their specific, though veiled references to the months of the Great Year, each of which could be described as an age, or aeon. In other words, it may have stopped us realising that when they spoke of the end of the age or series of ages, they could have been referring to the end of a "month" or a series of "months" of the Great Year.

Hermann Sasse's comprehensive analysis of the word *aiōn* in Kittel's *Theological Dictionary of the New Testament*,[1] gives this idea more weight than might be expected. After explaining its different meanings as "from eternity" and "to eternity", "for ever" and "never", especially in John's gospel, "the eternity of God" and "the duration of the world", he then goes on to link it with the theory of eternal recurrence and astrological ages:

If *aiōn* means the time or duration of the world, and the plural is firmly established, there is an obvious suggestion that the *aiōn* is not unique, but that there is a series of *aiōnes* in which all things flow in eternal recurrence. On this view, creation and conclusion are not to be taken in the sense of absolute beginning and end but rather in the sense of transition from one aeon to the other . . . This is the doctrine of eternity found in oriental astrology with its thought of eternal recurrence. It can hardly be doubted that this view had some influence on that of the Bible, especially on its eschatological ideas.[2]

This eschatological interpretation of "age" and "ages", being related to astrological epochs, suggests that they may indeed have corresponded to the "months" of the Great Year. Also, the interpretation of creation and conclusion as not being absolute but relative to the "transition from one aeon to the other", confirms my argument.

This evidence from Kittel also allows us to introduce the dimension of cosmic time into our understanding of two more New Testament references which use the Greek words *kairos* meaning specific time, and *chronos*, meaning time as a whole. These texts are associated with the notion of "the fullness of time" (*to plerōma tou chronou*, or *tōn kairōn*). The first is *Galatians* 4:4 "But when the time had fully come, God sent forth his Son" and the second is *Ephesians* 1:10 "according to his purpose which he set forth in Christ as a plan for the fullness of time, to unite all things in him". For the first the *Jerusalem Bible* gives "but when the appointed time came" and the second "when the times had run their course to the end". Other translations indicate the same sense that by "the fullness of time" is meant a specific moment which is both right for Christ to come and right because a cycle or age of time has been completed and a new one is ready to begin. This concept has a much more positive attitude to the times than those associated with "the last days" and brings out yet another aspect of New Testament time-consciousness which we can now see in a cosmic dimension. We may say from these texts that there was a belief not only that an age or series of ages was ending but that another age was beginning, and that beginning was associated with the coming of Jesus Christ.

Jesus and the Apocalyptic Tradition

We noted above that the *A.V.* translation of *aiōnōn* and *aiōn*, as "world" rather than "ages" or "age" in certain texts, had given to the New Testament a much greater sense of impending catastrophe hanging over it than was warranted. What a relief to know that for "end of the world" we can now, in these texts, (as modern translations show) read "end of the age"! Nevertheless there was a definite strand of biblical thought which *did* appear to believe that not just the age, but also the world, was about to end. There are a number of passages like *2 Peter* 2:8-13 which say in terms suggestive of nuclear war that "the heavens will be kindled and dissolved, and the elements will melt with fire". Texts of this type which grip the imagination most are those which report Jesus himself when he speaks of the end being nigh. The most arresting and controversial of these is in *Matthew* 16:28: "Truly I say to you, there are some standing here who will not taste death before they see the Son of man coming in his kingdom". It is sayings such as these which have led many scholars, most notably Albert Schweitzer, to assume that because the end of the world did *not* take place: "Jesus had after all been mistaken. The Kingdom he expected had never come".[3] However, difficult though it may be to understand what exactly he *did* mean, most of us would not wish to interpret such texts so negatively.

It is in *Matthew* 24 and related passages in *Mark* and *Luke* that we get the most extensive soliloquy on "the End" in which all the world's future travails are listed: "And you will hear of wars and rumours of wars; see that you are not alarmed; for this must take place, but *the end* is not yet" (vv. 6f). If these woes are analysed it appears that Jesus is speaking about two different but complementary types of "end". The first is that of the coming

81

destruction of Jerusalem and is associated with the prophecies that the Roman eagle – "the desolating sacrilege," – would stand in the holy place (*Matthew* 24:15), that Jerusalem would be surrounded by armies (*Luke* 21:20), that not one stone of the temple would be left upon another (*Matthew* 24:2) and that the Jews would "be led captive among all nations" (*Luke* 21:24). All these things did indeed take place in 70 AD. As Albert Nolan comments in *Jesus before Christianity*,"There can be no doubt that Jesus did prophesy the destruction of Jerusalem by the Romans"[4] and "What Jesus had to say about the last day was not apocalyptic, it was prophetic."[5]

The second is that of the literal end of the world as already indicated. In the light of our researches, I propose that Jesus was talking not about the end of the cosmos but about the end of the *age*. It is interesting to consider how many of his eschatological sayings can be explained either as prophecies concerning the imminent collapse of the state of Judea, or as expressions of his awareness of the turmoils that would inevitably accompany the ending of one cosmic age and the beginning of another. Indeed, it is so interesting that I believe that these two aspects of the historical process, the national and the cosmic, were the main factors which gave rise to the whole apocalyptic tradition.

Turning to a standard textbook on what is called the Inter-Testamental period, *The Jews from Alexander to Herod* by D.S.Russell, this is precisely what we find. Speaking about the rise of apocalyptic literature from 165 BC., he says that the profusion of insights which flourished from that time until the end of the first century AD., "were inspired by the troublous times in which the Jewish people were then living, first under the Seleucids and then under the Romans".[6] Regarding our second possible reason for the rise of apocalyptic visions of the End, namely the imminent ending of a cosmic age, or ages, he is equally positive, although he does say that the prophetic phrase "the latter end of the days", which had been used to denote the end of an era, "now indicated not just the end of an historical era, but the end of history itself".[7] An indication that by "era" he means something calculated by the cycles of the heavenly bodies, is given when he is discussing the influence of Zoroastrianism and its teaching that world history could be divided up into four great epochs of 3,000 years each, which culminated in a golden age:

The historical events marking the divisions of history, it is claimed in these writings, are regulated by the movement of the heavenly bodies (cf *Jub.* 4:17,19 etc) and have been recorded in heavenly tablets (cf *Jub.* 1:29 etc), whose secrets God has now made known to the 'wise' among the people. The impression of 'foretelling' is strengthened by the writers' adoption, as pseudonyms, of the names of ancient worthies – ranging from Adam to Ezra – to whom the divine secrets, it is said, have been revealed, but which have been kept hidden until now. In this way they are able to relate history in terms of foretelling, and by the calculation of times and seasons to predict the date of the End. Such calculations play a big part in these writings, and make clear not only that the climax of history is at hand but also that there is the closest possible connection between the events of human history and the working out of the divine purpose.[8]

Russell goes on to point out that usually the apocalyptic belief in two ages was characterised by this present evil age which would pass away and "the age to come" in which evil would be destroyed for ever. This "age to come" was synonymous with the notion of "the Kingdom" which would be ushered in as a heaven on earth in which the righteous, victorious over all enemies, would rule with God.

But what is so intriguing from our point of view, is that the understanding of "two ages" seems to have been fundamental to the apocalyptic tradition and that the exact time of the End, or transition to "the age to come" was "regulated by the movement of the heavenly bodies".[9] Bearing in mind the extent to which we have seen that the New Testament writings were influenced by the apocalyptic tradition, it seems reasonable to suppose that the End-time texts were referring basically to this pervasive "two age" belief. Furthermore, it is equally reasonable to suppose that the New Testament writers were also aware that the numerous attempts to foretell the exact time of the End – or new beginning – were "regulated by the movement of the heavenly bodies". With this in mind, we can see a clear connection between our earlier discoveries about the number 72 in the Great Year and the "end of the age" thinking which is one of the main themes of the New Testament. Is there anything recorded in the life of Jesus that might show us clearly that the New Testament writers saw him specifically as the one who ushered in the end of one age and the beginning of the next? The answer to that must be in the affirmative, because of the likeness which New Testament apocalyptic bears to the Jewish tradition of apocalyptic as a whole. So the next question must be: is there anything recorded in the life of Jesus that indicates that his coming at the end of the age had been predicted exactly "by the movement of the heavenly bodies"? The answer once again is, yes, there is. In *Matthew* 2:1-12 we are told about wise men from the East who "came to Jerusalem, saying 'Where is he who has been born king of the Jews? For we have seen his star in the East, and we have come to worship him'". As C. G. Jung says in *Aion*, this story "proves that Christ, possibly even at the time of the apostles, was viewed from the astrological standpoint".[10] We must therefore now ask: what was "his star" and what did it have to do with the end of the age?

The Star of Bethlehem

David Hughes begins what must be the most comprehensive and authoritative modern study of this topic in *The*

Star of Bethlehem Mystery by asking the same question:

> What was the star of Bethlehem? Did it really exist? What does it tell us about the birth of Jesus? These questions have been asked throughout the ages and numerous answers have been given over the course of many centuries.[11]

He goes on to list the various celestial phenomena which the star has been thought to be:

> Above all, the star of Bethlehem is a mystery. If it did exist, then it is one of the most amazing phenomena ever witnessed by man. The flow of serious scientific works and popular articles on the star goes on unabated. Theories vary from a nova or supernova to a comet, from a conjunction of Saturn and Jupiter in the constellation of Pisces to Venus, quite apart from other explanations such as a fireball, zodiacal light, ball lightning and the variable star Mira. Even the possibility that the star was simply a legend has to be taken seriously. At the other extreme, an explanation in terms of a miracle beyond the scope of science also has its advocates.[12]

Hughes' book is a brilliant survey of all these possible theories, and it may be a source of some relief to know that we are not going to plod our way through them. Instead, we are going to go straight to his conclusion which, as it happens, turns out to be the interpretation which has been generally held down the centuries, especially since 1603, when the famous astronomer Kepler gave it increased scientific credibility. It is also the interpretation most favoured by contemporary biblical scholars:[13]

> Our conclusion is that the explanation of the star of Bethlehem lies in a tangible physical phenomenon ... the physical occurrence that made up the Star of Bethlehem was the series of conjunctions, the apparent coming together in the sky and accompanying risings and settings, of the major planets Jupiter and Saturn. This is not a new conclusion, in

fact it can be dated back over seven hundred years, but the movements of Saturn and Jupiter in Pisces fit the large majority of the facts. The Piscean conjunction is rare enough to have been considered unusual. This explanation also has the advantage that the Magi did not have to go continually across the desert for every nova, comet or fireball that happened to appear. It was possible to predict the conjunction, the Babylonian magi had done just that, as the cuneiform tablets testify. The phenomenon had an inherent astrological message which equated it directly with 'his star' (Matthew 2:2). No comet, nova, fixed star, fireball or whatever could justify this appellation. It was long-lasting, long enough to be seen when the Magi were in their own country, while they were on the journey and on the final leg from Jerusalem to Bethlehem. Historically it occurred at the right time in 7 BC. And finally, even though it was an extremely significant event to a trained astrologer, in reality it consisted of two perfectly normal planets moving as usual along their ordained celestial paths. That is why Herod and the people of Jerusalem could easily miss its significance.[14]

The star then, was no legend or miracle, but an actual astronomical occurrence and an ordinary, if rare, one at that. I have found Hughes' book most convincing and recommend it to all those who wish to follow the discussion in detail. Much the same conclusion is put forward in a popular and shorter account, by Werner Keller in *The Bible as History*.[15] He is most readable and makes the astronomical aspect easy to understand.

So the star of Bethlehem was most probably the series of conjunctions of Jupiter and Saturn in the constellation of Pisces around 7 B.C. We will leave aside the reasons why the Magi thought these particular conjunctions worth following,[16] and move on to answer the second part of our question, what did "his star" have to do with the end of the age as we have come to understand that and the other New Testament phrases relating to the "End-times"? Hughes himself gives us the first clue towards an answer when he says "perhaps the star was . . .

a sign marking the passage of one age and the dawn of another".[17] Keller hints even more openly "The constellation of Pisces stood at the end of the sun's old course and at the beginning of its new one. What is more likely than that they saw in it the sign of the end of an old age and the start of a new one?"[18]

These comments prompt the question: could it be that, when New Testament writers speak of "the end of the age", "the end of ages", "the last days", "the fullness of time", etc., they were really referring to what Hughes calls, "the passage of one age and the dawn of another" and Keller "the end of an old age and the start of another"? May we not legitimately connect what Russell has told us about the general apocalyptic tendency to predict the exact date of the End-time by observations of "the movement of the heavenly bodies" with the ancient science and art of astronomy-astrology? Since we have established that Jesus shared the eschatological consciousness of the apocalyptic tradition, should we not therefore link him also with this interpretation?

Giorgio de Santillana and Hertha von Dechend, quoted in the last chapter, have no doubt at all about this. For them the link is clear. The star of Bethlehem did indeed herald a new and blessed age, the age of Pisces:

But the coming of Pisces was long looked forward to, heralded as a blessed age. It was introduced by the thrice-repeated Great Conjunction of Saturn and Jupiter in Pisces in the year 6 BC, the star of Bethlehem. Virgil announced the return of the Golden Age under the rule of Saturn, in his famous Fourth Eclogue: "Now the Virgin returns, the reign of Saturn returns, now a new generation descends from heaven on high. Only do thou, pure Lucina, smile on the birth of the child, under whom the iron brood shall first cease, and a golden race spring up throughout the world!" Although promoted to the rank of a "Christian honoris causa" on account of this poem, Virgil was no "prophet", nor was he the only one who expected the return of Kronos-Saturn.[19]

Santillana and Dechend represent a wide spectrum of scholarship which appears to take for granted that the star of Bethlehem did have a direct relationship to the end of one age and the beginning of another. The age of Pisces was dawning. In another passage they go further and link the star directly with Christ, the Fish, saying "The advent of Christ the Fish marks our age".[20]

It would seem, then, from these authorities that what Virgil said in his famous *Fourth Eclogue*[21] was equivalent to what the apocalyptics were predicting as "the End-time" by observations of "the movement of the heavenly bodies". It would thus also appear that we are forging an unexpectedly strong link between the pervasive attitude to "the last days" in the New Testament and the ages or months of the Great Year.

Santillana and Dechend speak of the new age of Pisces dawning, but some scholars go further and say that a completely new Great Year was starting. In other words that the transition to Pisces was ending one complete cycle of 25,920 years and beginning another. If this was so then no wonder there was turmoil and an increasing belief in the apparent end of the whole world for, as Alan Oken says in *Astrology: Evolution and Revolution*, "when the Earth progresses into a new World Age, there is a precipitation of incoming energies which causes significant variations in terrestrial occurrences".[22] Oken is one of those who is convinced that not just a new age but a new Great Year began with Jesus, for he says "The transition to the first Age of a new Great Year was personified by the birth of Jesus".[23] If it was the dawn of not just a new age but a new Great Year then this would, along with all the political portents of doom already mentioned, almost totally explain the pervasive apocalyptic atmosphere which colours the whole of the New Testament writings.

But what precisely *is* a transition from one age to another, or more particularly from one Great Year to another, and how does it link in with the precession of the equinoxes as described in the last chapter? Vera Reid, in her history of the zodiacal ages *Towards Aquarius*, gives an explanation:

The transition between the ages of Aries and Pisces marked a turning point both in human evolution and in world history for it coincided with the close of one Great Year and the opening of another . . .
The zodiac is composed of twelve glyphs which may be considered as the formula of a sequential life-process applicable to every manifestation of life. Thus man is a microscopic circle whose members and organs reflect the cosmic macrocosm and the twelve divisions of the celestial zodiac. Following the traditional significance of the zodiacal glyphs, Aries, the first sign, governs the head, Taurus the throat and so on round the circle to Pisces, the twelfth sign symbolising the feet. In the lesser cycle of the common year (365 days) the sun appears to move through the celestial zodiac in the order of the signs . . . beginning with Aries the head and ending with Pisces the feet. In the 25,000 year cycle of the Great Year, however, the sun, owing to the precession of the equinoxes, appears to move in the reverse direction, that is, from the feet, Pisces, to the head, Aries. Thus, in either case, we may consider that a new cycle comes to birth between these two signs. . . In suggesting, therefore, that the Great New Year, or 25,000 year cycle, begins when the sun enters the sign of Pisces we are following the correspondence between the microcosm and the macrocosm.[24]

Thus it would appear from these authorities that we have established a strong case for maintaining that the star of Bethlehem marked not only the end of the age of Aries but also of a complete Great Year, and that it therefore also marked not only the beginning of the age of Pisces, but also of a whole new Great Year.

We now know what our New Testament writer might have answered when we asked him "What's the cosmic time please?" He surely would have had no hesitation in saying "Why, its New Year's Day of course – Great New Year's Day!" According to our calculations, Great New Year's Day began with the birth of Christ and lasted 72 years, until the fall of Jerusalem and destruction of the temple by the Romans. As Jesus foretold, it was indeed "the last day" and "the end of the world" for the Jews; but for the Christians, a new heaven and a new earth was being created.

CHAPTER 6

ICHTHUS: THE GREAT FISH

We have now reached something of a turning point in our enquiry. After considering the cosmic significance of the number 72 in chapter 4, we saw in the last chapter that it was no isolated coincidence that this number represented the number of years in one "day" of the Great Year. We also saw that it was part of a consciousness of "the End-time", a consciousness which pervaded the whole New Testament and which, through an examination of the Inter-Testamental apocalyptic tradition, we were able to link with the end, not only of a cosmic age or "month" but also of a complete Great Year. We saw too, in the star of Bethlehem, a very clear connection between the Great Year and the birth of Jesus Christ.

I want next to follow the star a little further, to see if we can discern any consciousness in the New Testament that the age of Aries was ending and that the age of Pisces was beginning. In other words, just as in the last chapter we considered the general New Testament attitude to "the times", so now I want to ask: are there any texts within the New Testament which suggest that there might have been an awareness that it was specifically the age of *Aries* that was ending and the age of *Pisces* beginning? Possible texts immediately spring to mind when we remember that Aries means Ram and Pisces means Fish.

The Ram-Lamb

C.H. Dodd in his authoritative work *The Interpretation of the Fourth Gospel* considers that in the New Testament

91

the words *amnos* and *arnion* (translated *lamb*) can also allude to a young horned ram. He holds that these Greek words appear to have been adopted by some Greek-speaking Christians as images of the Messiah – "the leader of the flock of God" – as well as images of the Passover sacrificial victim. He maintains that when John the Baptist said "Behold the Lamb of God who takes away the sin of the world" (*John* 1:29) he meant "God's messiah who makes an end of sin".[1] This famous Johannine text is, of course, just one of several in the New Testament which we have come to associate principally with the central doctrine of Christ's vicarious suffering on our behalf (cf *Acts* 8:32; *1 Cor* 5:7; *1 Peter* 1:19).

It is, however, by no means easy to demonstrate that the symbol of the Lamb in the New Testament had any astrological significance. It is all very well to imply, because the Messiah's death as sacrificial Lamb of God coincided with the end of the age of Aries, that the New Testament writers were aware, as Kenneth Cuming asserts in *God and the New Age*, that Christ had "brought to an end the Age of Aries the Ram by becoming the living symbol in Himself".[2] But what justification have we got for this inference? Just because the whole concept of the lamb of sacrifice coincided with the Arian age, it does not necessarily mean that this was more than a coincidence. Similarly just because the sacrifice of lambs did in fact end a generation after Jesus died, when the temple was destroyed, it does not necessarily follow that these events were in any way connected.

The Fish

It is equally hard to prove, just because there are 28 passages in the gospels which refer to fish, that they necessarily indicate that the writers wished to tell us in sign language that the Piscean age had begun. After all, it is reasonable to assume that disciples who were selected from villages around the Sea of Galilee, would have had more than a passing interest in the fish-trade, even if not all of them were themselves fishermen; and that this alone could account for many, if not all, of the "fish" texts in the gospels. What cosmic significance, for instance, can we with any credibility extrapolate from *Luke* 24:24 where we are told that when the resurrected Jesus asked his disciples "Have you anything here to eat?", they "gave him a piece of broiled fish, and he took and ate before them"? It seems ludicrous to imply from this that they gave Jesus a piece of broiled fish because he was the great Fisherman of the new Piscean age! It was as natural for them to happen to have some fish on the broil as for us to heat up something out of the freezer.

Yet having said this, and after making all due allowances for the scepticism which naturally arises in minds which have been taught by the Church[3] and by science[4] to be dismissive of all astrological inferences, there is another area of evidence to which we should now turn. This is an area which is not so easy to dismiss, which does imply that the New Testament writers were most probably well aware of the link between the fish and Pisces. I refer to the symbolism of the Early Church.

Ichthus in the Early Church

The Christian symbol of the fish first appeared in Alexandria around 200 AD.,and William Neil in *The Christian Faith in Art* says that thereafter it became so important that it was recognised as *the* Christian sign, summing up all the important doctrines of the faith:

The sacramental symbols of Baptism as the beginning of the new life of the Christian, and of the Eucharist as a dramatization of the Passion and Resurrection, are summed up by the quasi-Biblical imagery of the Fish which features so largely in early Christian painting. The letters of the Greek word for fish, *ichthus*, were ingeniously seen to be the initial letters of the Greek words 'Jesus Christ, Son of God,

Saviour' and to the Christians of the second century no symbol said so much. It stood for Incarnation, Redemption, Resurrection – the whole scheme of Christian salvation.[5]

After listing all these profound and comprehensive meanings of the symbol of the fish, Neil in the next sentence goes on to say that the fish became so important because "it was historically linked with the miracle of the Loaves and Fishes and the apostolic vocation to become 'fishers of men'".[6] At first glance these two biblical references would seem to give sufficient reason for the central importance of the fish to second-century Christians. But are they really? Are these and the other fishy texts enough to have made this sign become *the* expression of "Incarnation, Redemption, Resurrection – the whole scheme of Christian salvation"? I don't think so. I believe there would have to have been an even more profound meaning for this sign to have virtually taken over the faith and become *the* icon of the Early Church. This deeper, universal meaning from which all the other references took their added significance, I believe, could only have been that of the Piscean age.

Gilbert Cope, in the chapter "Early Christian Art" in *Symbolism in the Bible and in the Church*, has a section which amplifies Neil. He lists the different meanings of the fish symbol:

In early Christian art a Fish, in the first place, signifies the soul of the departed; secondly it signifies the eucharistic spiritual food; thirdly it signifies the presence of Christ himself, for very early it had been noticed that the letters of the Greek word for fish – I-Ch-Th-U-S – acrostically provided the initials for Jesus-Christ-of God-Son-Saviour. The Fish, in the early Christian centuries, was therefore a very powerful symbol indeed.[7]

Like Neil, Cope explains the importance of the fish by referring to the variety of New Testament texts:

In the Gospels there is a great deal about boats and fishing: several of the disciples were fishermen, Jesus travelled in and preached from a boat, he stilled a storm and walked on water, he spoke of 'fishers of men', he referred to Jonah in the whale's belly as a type of his resurrection (Matthew 12:39f) and to Noah's flood as a type of his resurrection (Matthew 12:39f) and to Noah's flood as a type of the *eschaton* (Luke 17:26-30), fishes were eaten at the eucharistic meals when the crowds were fed, there was a coin in a fish's mouth, after the seven disciples had caught 153 the Risen Lord gave them fish and bread to eat (John 21:1f).[8]

But are these texts enough to account for the sustained ascendancy of the fish over other symbols such as the lamb or the light? Edward Hulme is one who does not think so. In *Symbolism in Christian Art*, he finds it inexplicable and objectionable:

It is somewhat curious that such a symbol (the fish) should have held its ground so long, since it sprang merely from a verbal or rather a literal coincidence, and that too of a somewhat forced nature. It had nothing of the poetical feeling of that beautiful symbol, the Lamb, nor did it express like the lion, anything of the royal majesty of the great King of kings. The form was based on no allusion in any text, and the difference and distance between the cold-blooded and apathetic creature of the waters and the Creator, the Lord of all, who suffered so freely for the sheep of His pasture, is something infinitely great, and would, we should have thought, have led men earlier to feel how unworthy the symbol was of One so infinitely tender, One so immeasurably exalted.[9]

Hulme's sentiments are, I believe, thoroughly understandable. The "cold-blooded and apathetic creature of the waters" symbolising the infinitely tender and exalted Saviour. How inappropriate! What have they in common? Surely nothing at all. I am so sympathetic to this position that I suggest that the whole thing *is* inexplicable unless we see in it the underlying reference to the Piscean age. After all, why should it interest the early Church quite so much that the Greek word for fish spelt out the initials of Jesus – Christ – Son of God – Saviour? So what? Surely Hulme is right when he says that this is merely a "verbal, or rather literal coincidence, and that too of a somewhat forced nature". For nowhere in the New Testament is Jesus himself ever referred to as the Fish. The lamb, the light of the world, the bread of life, the door of the sheep etc, yes, – but never the Fish. How else can we explain that not only did the fish become *the* symbol of the faith for the Early Church but also actually symbolised the person of Jesus himself? *Ichthus* symbolised Jesus Christ, not just the sum of Christian doctrine, and this was evidently the case as much for the Early Church Fathers as for the iconographers.

Writing in the third century, Tertullian says "we little fishes, following the example of our Fish Jesus Christ, are born in water".[10] A third century Christian tombstone at Autun states "Divine offspring of the heavenly Fish ..."[11] and Bishop Abercius of Hieropolis around 200 AD., speaking of the eucharistic bread, said "set before me for food the Fish ... whom a spotless Virgin caught".[12] These and other early Christian writers saw Christ himself as the Fish. The Fish for them had supplanted all other New Testament images as a symbol of all doctrine *and* of Jesus himself. I must confess that I cannot see any justification for the dominance of this image over the other legitimate New Testament metaphors other than the pervasive consciousness that Christ's birth had ushered in the new age of Pisces and that the new spiritual energies associated with him were somehow also associated with a specifically Piscean spirituality.

This is the opinion of Herbert Whone in *Church, Monastery, Cathedral*. Under the paragraph *Fish*, he writes:

The fish as a symbol is closely connected with Christ. In the early Church he was called Iesous Ichthus (Jesus the Fish) or sometimes 'the Great Fish'. This was because Christ's birth heralded the beginning of the zodiacal era of 2150 years, the Sign of Pisces (The Fishes).[13]

Whone then goes on to speak about a specifically Piscean spirituality:

> The Piscean Era has much to do with the washing away of impurity, with renunciation and suffering, in order to make way for the new cycle of spiritual awareness, the Age of Aquarius. In terms of the individual, the image of the fish suggests the material and psychic sea in which a man flounders. But it is Christ, descending into this sea, embracing all men in an act of sacrificial redemption, that shows the opposite face of Pisces. And man's confusion in the sea is redeemed by his own developing capacity for love and compassion.[14]

It seems, then, that an examination of the New Testament texts which refer to fish does not in itself justify us in our coming to the conclusion that they had any explicit astrological significance. However, now that we have looked into the evidence of the Early Church, it does appear that we would be justified in agreeing with Herbert Whone. We can corroborate his position from the conclusion we came to in the last chapter regarding the apocalyptic tradition and the star of Bethlehem. We accepted that "his star" was most probably the series of conjunctions of Jupiter and Saturn in the constellation of Pisces. We can now understand that the new ascendancy of the constellation of Pisces would be the most likely reason why the followers of Jesus pictured him as the Great Fish even though he was not so designated in the New Testament. We can now also understand that, as Whone points out, the qualities we associate with him, ie. washing away of impurity, renunciation, suffering and compassion, were specifically Piscean attributes and that therefore the fish would also inevitably come to be seen as symbolising "Incarnation, Redemption, Resurrection – the whole scheme of Christian salvation".

Indeed, I think we can, on the principle of "as above, so below", go so far as to accept the increased influence of the constellation of Pisces as the most likely explanation of why the symbol of the fish gained such an ascendancy within Christianity in the centuries after the New Testament canon was closed. Consequently, we should now have serious reservations about agreeing with Edward Hulme that it is "somewhat curious that such a symbol should have held its ground so long".

The Vesica Piscis in Sacred Geometry

There is another department of traditional symbolism which has always assumed a fundamental connection between Jesus Christ and the Piscean age. This is the ancient art-science of sacred geometry which we encountered in relation to the New Jerusalem and Solomon's temple. The specific geometrical figure to which both Christ and the fish are related is what is known as the *vesica piscis*, the vessel or bladder of the fish. This is the lozenge or almond shape formed by two interpenetrating circles whose centres lie on each other's circumference.

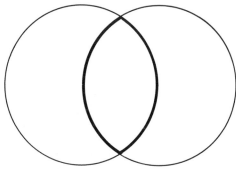

21 *The* vesica piscis

Herbert Whone explains the profound significance of this simple figure which is also known as the mandorla, the Italian word for almond:

The mandorla is the almond-shaped line drawn around the full-length figure of Christ, usually with fine lines radiating outwards from the body, showing the perfected inner light of divinity ... The mandorla is associated with Christ in majesty, though later, in medieval times, it became common to depict the Virgin Mary in the same way. Another name for it is the 'mystic almond'.

The image of the almond is a reference to the fruit of the tree which by its form suggests the womb, thus the womb of the world from which all developed and within which the redemptive power of Christ operates. The almond tree is itself associated with purity of birth ...

The mandorla is also known as the *vesica piscis* (Latin, 'bladder of the fish'), again an image of the waters of the womb of the world within which the Christ power radiates. In this sense Christ is the 'Great Fish' in the sea, having descended into that sea to redeem floundering humanity. Sometimes the mandorla is referred to as an *ichthus*, Greek 'fish', and again simply as the 'aureole'. It is exclusively the property of Christ and the Virgin.[15]

Whone here brings together the complementary meanings of the *vesica piscis*, ie. the bladder of the fish, the mandorla and the almond. It is surprising to find ourselves back to the fruit of the almond tree which, as we discovered in our examination of the seven-branch candlesticks in the temple, was the tree of life for the Hebrews. Perhaps it was given this pre-eminence as much for its womb-shaped fruit and importance in sacred geometry as for its beautiful early blossom. Whether this was the case or not, it is obvious that the almond shape does look like a womb and that this association was more than metaphorical. For just as Whone says it suggested "the womb of the world from which all developed", so according to John Michell, it is a geometrical fact that it is "the womb from which are generated all the numbers and ratios of the Temple".[16]

Robert Lawlor agrees, saying "The Vesica is also a form

generator in that all the regular polygons can be said to arise from the succession of vesica constructions".[17]

22 *Christ within the* vesica

Is it once more fortuitous or, as Edward Hulme might say, "a literal coincidence, and that too of a somewhat forced nature", that the womb-like shape, the geometric importance, the association with Christ and the Piscean age all come together in this figure? Is it also a coincidence that from early in the Piscean age, the bishop's mitre "assumed the shape of a fish-head with reference to

23 *The* vesica piscis *as bishop's mitre*

Christ who was known to the early Christians as the Great Fish"?[18]

Whone, Michell and Lawlor do not think so. Lawlor is particularly explicit about the link between the *vesica*, Christ and the age of Pisces:

The overlapping circles – an excellent representation of a cell, or any unity in the midst of becoming dual – form a fish-shaped central area which is one source of the symbolic reference to Christ as a fish. Christ, as universal function, is symbolically this region which joins together heaven and earth, above and below, creator and creation. The fish is also the symbolic designation of the Piscean Age, and consequently the Vesica is the dominant geometrical figure for this period of cosmic and human evolution, and is the major thematic source for the cosmic temples of this age in the west, the Gothic cathedral. Jesus as the centre of the Vesica carries the idea of the non-substantial, universal 'Christic' principle entering into the manifest world of duality and form. The Piscean Age has been characterized as that of the formal embodiment of spirit, manifesting a deeper penetration of spirit into form, with a concurrent deepening of the materialization of spirit: the Word becomes flesh.[19]

Enough has now been said in this and the previous chapter to substantiate the proposition that in the New Testament writings implicitly and in the Early Church explicitly, there was a pervasive consciousness that Jesus Christ was not only the Saviour from sin, the Redeemer of the individual soul, but that he was also the embodiment of a specifically Piscean spirituality. There would appear to be sufficient evidence to maintain that there was a widespread realisation that a new age had begun in and through him and that the eternal Word which had become flesh had done so as *ichthus*, the Great Fish.

We are at last, I believe, coming to a position from which we can begin to look at the Bible and some traditional Chrisitan presuppositions from a new perspective. This is the perspective of the Great Year, each age or "month" of which as we have seen is approximately 2,160 years long. Once we learn to view the panorama of the ages rising and falling according to these "months", then a new way of relating our faith and the Bible to the historical process opens up to us. We can begin to chart our own position in relation to this process and begin also to understand precisely *why* the millenarian literalists we mentioned in the first chapter, have got it wrong. For just as the traditional interpretation of New Testament apocalyptic mistook the end of the *age* for the end of the *world*, so today many who espouse Armageddon theology are doing the same. It may be that we too, although we may shun all forms of millenarianism, are not doing any better because we have not yet seen how an understanding of the ages of the Great Year can change our pessimistic agnosticism about the future, into a hope in the age to come. The age to come two thousand years ago was that of Pisces. Today it is that of Aquarius.

We have now established beyond any reasonable doubt that the writers of the New Testament believed Jesus Christ had universal and cosmic significance. Understanding this can help us interpret the signs of *our* times and find hope for *our* future. It is in the context of the ages of the Great Year that I believe this can be done, for it is not the world which is going to end soon but it is the age – the age of Pisces. There are great changes taking place because, as Alan Oken has told us, "When the Earth progresses into a new World Age, there is a precipitation of incoming energies which causes significant variations in terrestrial occurrences". If you were asked "What's the cosmic time please?" what would you answer? Did you know that, according to the precession of the equinoxes, the age of Pisces will soon be ending, and that this is the dawning of the age of Aquarius?

CHAPTER 7

AQUARIUS: THE SPIRIT POURER

We now come to a consideration of the age of Aquarius which, according to many accounts, is dawning in our time. As the famous song from *Hair* asserted so emphatically, "This is the dawning of the age of Aquarius". In the last chapter we looked for New Testament texts and Early Church symbols which showed that there was a general awareness that the age of Pisces had begun. Now we are similarly going to look for evidence of Aquarian symbolism. After all, if it really is the beginning, or nearly the beginning of a new age, then there should be something about it – and indeed about all future ages – pre-figured in the New Testament. It would be a terrible thing if we had to go into the Aquarian age still clutching our old Piscean symbols.

The Man carrying a Jar of Water

At first it would seem a tall order. Aquarian symbolism in the Bible seems an unlikely proposition. Remembering that Aquarius is the Water Carrier we could, of course, ask ourselves whether we can think of any text in the gospels which refers to a water-carrier. One obvious one comes to mind: *Mark* 14:13 (cf. *Luke* 22:10) where Jesus, in the course of giving his disciples instructions regarding the preparations for the Last Supper, said:

> Go into the city, and a man carrying a jar of water will meet you; follow him, and wherever he enters, say to the householder, 'The teacher says, Where is my guest room,

where am I to eat the passover with my disciples?' And he will show you a large upper room furnished and ready; there prepare for us.

This story is a favourite one among astrologers hunting for Aquarian texts.[1] It is referred to as the foreshadowing of the age after Pisces, for instance by Peter Lemesurier in *Gospel of the Stars*, who sees the whole of the Last Supper as symbolic of the millennial banquet:

. . . the pilgrims of humanity will be met by a man carrying a pitcher of water. Not the woman whose normal task it was. But a man. A man thereby identifies himself.
As Aquarius.
And as the celestial water-carrier comes to meet them, they in turn must follow him. To an upper room. A large upper room, already prepared.
'I go to prepare a place for you.' said Jesus. 'And if I go and prepare a place for you, I shall come again and receive you to myself, so that where I am you may be also.'
And now, in symbol, that moment had come.
For there, in that large upper room which represents the limitless higher planes, the exalted dimensions of the coming Millennium, a feast had been prepared. The Passover-supper, the Messianic Banquet which throughout the prophecies had never ceased to symbolise the future Golden Age . . .[2]

I do not doubt that this "man carrying a jar of water" could possibly be a symbol of Aquarius. Nor do I doubt that once you have made up your mind that he *is* Aquarius, the upper room may well become symbolic of the millennial banquet. Nevertheless, the overall impression I am left with is that Lemesurier's imagination is a little too lively and that his symbolic interpretation has gone a bit over the top. It is too easy to turn the gospel stories into allegories and I would need more than this one man carrying a water jar in order to be convinced that Aquarius is in the New Testament. It is not that I think Lemesurier and those who follow this interpretation are necessarily wrong. It is just that they make too much of it. I am not convinced that this text *is* the main one we are looking for. After all, there were twenty-eight texts which spoke about fish for the Piscean age. Surely there ought to be more than one which speaks about water-carriers for the Aquarian. Where can they be found?

The Out-Pouring of the Spirit

Looking at pictorial representations of Aquarius, you will notice two things which I believe are important in the quest for possible Aquarian texts. The first is that the

24 *Aquarius as water pourer*

106

Water Carrier is usually pictured *pouring* his water out, never just *carrying* it. He is seldom drawn as "a man carrying a jar of water", but very often as a man pouring a jar of water. He is not so much a water carrier as a water pourer. The second is that he is always pictured as being up in the air, pouring his water down onto the earth. When we also realise that, according to Vera Reid, the water which he is pouring "is not the water of the earth" but "the Water of Life"[3], we are ready to redefine our question: can we think of any New Testament texts which speak about the Water of Life being poured out from the sky onto the earth? Well, there is one which leaps to mind if by "Water of Life" is meant something like the Spirit. This is the famous one from the prophet Joel, quoted by Peter (*Acts* 2:17-18) to justify the strange phenomena of speaking in tongues, which had just broken out amongst the disciples on the day of Pentecost, ten days after Jesus' ascension and fifty after his resurrection, when he said:

... but this is what was spoken by the prophet Joel:
'And in the last days it shall be, God declares,
that I will pour out my Spirit upon all flesh,
and your sons and daughters shall prophesy,
and your young men shall see visions,
and your old men shall dream dreams;
yea, and on my menservants and my maidservants in those days
I will pour out my Spirit; and they shall prophesy'.

The expression "I will pour out", is only a figure of speech in Joel's prophecy and is used in several other contexts in the New Testament.[4] Nevertheless it seems to have been integral to the way in which the disciples described their experience of the Spirit at Pentecost. Luke refers to it again in exactly the same way in *Acts* 2:33, and 10:45. Speaking of the Gentile Pentecost which came later, he said "the gift of the Holy Spirit had been poured out even on the Gentiles".

Unlike the "man carrying the jar of water," these two texts are of supreme importance in the New Testament because they describe the first Pentecost, which is usually thought of as the birthday of the Jewish Church, and the second "Pentecost" which began the Gentile Church. In both, the image used of the Spirit is that it was "poured out".[5] The "man carrying a jar of water" led the disciples to the upper room but disappeared into the shadows without a word, still_carrying his jar of earthly water. But at Pentecost the waters of life were not merely carried across the stage of history, they were actually *poured out*. I believe it is these two texts, which may be legitimately taken to be symbolic of Aquarius, because of their metaphorical appropriateness and central importance. This is further borne out if we look more closely at the story of Pentecost.

The Baptism in the Holy Spirit

This pouring out of the Spirit at Pentecost is also called the "baptism in the Holy Spirit". Just before his ascension Jesus told his disciples not to depart from Jerusalem, but to wait for the promise of the Father, which, he said "you heard from me, for John baptized with water, but before many days you shall be baptized with the Holy Spirit" (*Acts* 1:4-5). Jesus' reference to John the Baptist drew the distinction between his own baptism in the Holy Spirit and John's baptism in water. This occurred at the beginning of his ministry, at the time when John had testified in these terms: "I saw the Spirit descend as a dove from heaven, and it remained on him. I myself did not know him; but he who sent me to baptize with water said to me, 'He on whom you see the Spirit descend and remain, this is he who baptizes with the Holy Spirit'" (*John* 1:32). This text is recorded in all four gospels; *Matthew* and *Luke* add that Jesus would baptize "with the Holy Spirit *and with fire*".

It is an extraordinary fact that throughout the Christian era, apart from the reference to "he breathed on them, and said to them 'Receive the Holy Spirit'" (*John* 20:22), at Anglican and Catholic Confirmation services, this baptism with the Holy Spirit has gone largely unnoticed. It hardly features at all as a distinctive doctrine or article of faith. By contrast however, baptism in water has not only featured prominently, but has also been the subject of bitter and heated theological controversy – and still is. The Catholics and the Anglo-Catholics for instance believe in what is known as baptismal regeneration, ie. that the action of baptising by sprinkling the head with water actually confers the grace of salvation, the washing away of sins through the blood of Christ. The Baptists on the other hand are a distinctive denomination largely because they believe in baptism for believers only by total immersion. To be a Christian in almost any denomination means making up your mind not on *whether* but on *how* important water baptism is, whereas baptism in the Holy Spirit is scarcely ever mentioned.

If baptism in the Holy Spirit is so important in the New Testament, how is it that it has been neglected throughout church history? If John the Baptist implied that his water baptism for the remission of sins was as nothing compared to Jesus' Spirit baptism, how can we explain that the churches have been so totally taken up with the former but not with the latter? Could the answer possibly be that throughout the Piscean age anything to do with the symbolism of water took precedence over anything to do with air? The fishes swim in water. Pisces is a water sign. They will only take their air through water, never through the air or they die – like fish out of water. By contrast Aquarius is an air sign. He lives up in the air and the "water" he pours out is the airy world of the Spirit. It should follow then that if we are moving towards the Aquarian age, and if our New Testament "Aquarian" textual interpretations are on the right lines, we might expect Spirit baptism to be becoming more important and water baptism less so. Strangely enough, while it might be difficult to substantiate the latter, the former is most definitely the case, as anyone who has had dealings with the Pentecostal and Charismatic movements knows.

The Pentecostals and Charismatics

It is a startling fact of ecclesiastical life today that all over the world Christians are having the experience of what they call the "baptism in the Holy Spirit" as on the first day of Pentecost. The Pentecostal Churches number millions and so now do the Charismatics, that is to say, the Pentecostals *within* the historic denominations. It is a remarkable phenomenon, and it is a uniquely twentieth-century one. At a time when we speak of the "post-christian age" and the "secular world", the Pentecostals, since their beginnings in 1900, have consistently experienced an exponential rate of growth.[6] How can we understand this when many other churches are in decline? Could it be that, as the Piscean age wanes and the Aquarian age begins, so Christ is manifesting himself in his new role as Aquarius the Spirit Pourer who, "baptizes in the Holy Spirit"? Not that he wasn't always this from the first Pentecost, but it is only now "in the fullness of time" that this particular aspect of his person and work can be received.

In the light of what has been said earlier about the numbers 70 and 72, it is notable that 70 years before the Pentecostal movement began, there was a mini-Pentecost which pre-figured the twentieth-century out-pouring in almost every respect. This was the revival in the early 1830's in the west of Scotland and London, associated with the name of Edward Irving, which developed into the denomination known as the Catholic Apostolic Church.[7]

Irving was a famous preacher in London and was the

first theologian since Tertullian in the early third century,[8] to speak and write about the baptism in the Holy Spirit as a distinctive doctrine. He wrote a tract called *The Day of Pentecost, or the Baptism with the Holy Ghost* in which he taught that the experience of Pentecost was the birthright of every believer.[9] Why did so many centuries have to pass before such an obvious and central doctrine could be rediscovered and proclaimed? This was something he wondered about himself:

> But what then are we to make of our fathers, who knew little or nothing of this [the baptism in the Holy Spirit], and had no marks of possessing it; nor the Reformers; nor the saints and martyrs later than the third century? I have given thee rest on this question. They might still have regeneration and remission, and the grace of both sacraments: but God is leading us of this age back to fountains of which our fathers never drank; which were open to them indeed, as to the first Christians, but the way unto them was not known.[10]

Why was it that the way back to these living fountains was only discovered in 1830? Could it be that the God who "is leading us of this age back to fountains of which our fathers never drank" was the God and Father, not only of the Great Fish, but of the Water Carrier, the Spirit Pourer? After all, 1830 years out of the allotted 2,160 years of the age of the Great Fish had passed. 1830 stood at 25.5 degrees to 30 degrees of Pisces. Over 5/6th of the Piscean "month" had gone. All across the nation, there was a new vibration. New awarenesses were emerging. New symbols were assuming power. Old ones were becoming superannuated. Perhaps it was more than a coincidence that almost exactly one "day" later in the Piscean "month" in 1900, the Spirit Pourer began to manifest himself in that way again.

If Edward Irving may thus be regarded as the forerunner of this particular understanding of Aquarian spirituality, then his close friend and fellow native of

Annandale, Thomas Carlyle, may perhaps be thought of as the precursor of those such as Sir James Frazer in *The Golden Bough*, Carl Jung in *Aion*, Joseph Campbell in *The Masks of God* and Erich Neumann in *The Great Mother* who have since made comparative studies of the rise and fall of religious myths and symbols. Published in 1835, the year after Irving's untimely death, *Sartor Resartus* (literally "the tailor patched") is a witty and profound parable about the superannuation of symbols seen in the metaphor of clothes that wear out, as W. H. Hudson points out in the introduction to the *Everyman's Library* edition:

> All dogmas, forms and ceremonials, he teaches are but religious vestments – symbols expressing man's deepest sense of the divine mystery of the universe and the hunger and thirst of the soul for God. It is in response to the imperative necessities of his nature that he moulds for himself these outward emblems of his ideas and aspirations. Yet they are only emblems; and since, like all other human things, they partake of the ignorance and weakness of the times in which they were framed, it is inevitable that with the growth of knowledge and the expansion of thought they must presently be outgrown. When this happens, there follows what Carlyle calls the "superannuation of symbols". Men wake up to the fact that the creeds and formulas which have come down to them from the past are no longer living for them, no longer what they need for the embodiment of their spiritual life.[11]

There are many passages of *Sartor Resartus* which could be quoted as examples of this, but from our point of view, one about the Church is very apposite because it speaks not only of the present "out-at-elbows" clothes, but also of the future "new vestures" which are being secretly woven:

> Meanwhile, in our era of the World, those same Church-Clothes have gone sorrowfully out-at-elbows; nay far worse, many of them have become mere hollow Shapes, or

Masks, under which no living Figure or Spirit any longer dwells; but only spiders and unclean beetles, in horrid accumulation, drive their trade; and the mask still glares on you with its glass-eyes, in ghastly affectation of Life – some generation-and-half after Religion has quite withdrawn from it, and in unnoticed nooks is weaving for herself new Vestures, wherewith to reappear, and bless us, or our sons or grandsons.[12]

Although Carlyle does not tell us exactly what symbols have become superannuated and what are the new "masks of God", all that he says in terms of those "clothes" which are either "out-at-elbows" or being secretly woven into "new Vestures", runs parallel to Irving's God who is "leading us of this age back to fountains of which our fathers never drank". It also fits the basic astrological belief that, as Liz Greene puts it in *Relating*:

At the close of an era, many old gods die or are subordinated, and new gods – gods who are symbolic of energies which have not emerged into human consciousness before – are born[13]. . . What man worships as the highest possible ideal, the highest good and the highest mystery behind life, appears to be in some way symbolised by the governing astrological sign, and this mystery always embodies something entirely new, something previously unknown to man's consciousness.[14]

There is another aspect of *Sartor Resartus* in which Carlyle parallels Irving and in which he may perhaps be seen as an Aquarian prophet. This is in his experience of "conversion" in the *Rue Saint-Thomas de l'Enfer*. In the guise of his hero, Diogenes Teufelsdröckh, Carlyle describes how one day he confronted all his despair and fears and defied them, with astonishing effect:

Thus had the EVERLASTING NO (*das ewige Nein*) pealed authoritatively through all the recesses of my Being, of my ME; and then it was that my whole ME stood up, in native

God-created majesty, and with emphasis recorded its Protest. Such a Protest, the most important transaction in Life, may that same Indignation and Defiance, in a psychological point of view, be fitly called. The Everlasting No had said: "Behold, thou art fatherless, outcast, and the Universe is mine (the Devil's)"; to which my whole Me now made answer: "I am not thine, but Free, and forever hate thee!"

It is from this hour that I incline to date my Spiritual New-Birth, or Baphometic Fire-Baptism; perhaps I directly thereupon began to be a Man.[15]

What is important to notice in this famous account of how the "Everlasting No" began to change into the "Everlasting Yea", is the symbolism of baptism which Carlyle uses to describe it. We may take the word "Baphometic" to mean no more than "mysterious" since it is derived from a mythical androgenous icon, the Baphomet.[16] But fire baptism is not such an arcane concept since it comes directly from *Matthew* 3:11 and *Luke* 3:16, quoted above, "he will baptize you with the Holy Spirit *and with fire*". So even the doubting Thomas, while rejecting the out-at-elbows calvinism of his parents, could not stop himself describing this "most important transaction in Life" in terms of baptism – not the water baptism of the Church but the fire baptism which is so closely linked to the Spirit baptism that most commentators take it to be part of the same thing.[17] Obviously it would have been inappropriate for him to have used a phrase which had a well-known Christian meaning. Why then should he have called it a "Fire-baptism"? And why, for that matter, should *Matthew* and *Luke* have added "and with fire"? It is usually assumed that the answer to the latter lies in its association with the spiritual winnowing that would involve the chaff being burned "with unquenchable fire" (*Matthew* 3:12; *Luke* 3:17).[18] While this is undoubtedly the case, it may also perhaps, in the context of our present study, be taken to represent

114

Leo, the polar opposite, or complementary sign, of Aquarius. Although this may sound unlikely at first, we must remember that in astrological theory, it is held that the signs of the zodiac come in pairs of opposites. Thus the age of Pisces, to be more correct, is the age of Pisces-Virgo since Virgo, the Virgin, is the complementary sign of the Fish. Virgo is an earth-sign whose attributes balance those of the watery Pisces. Likewise, to be completely accurate, we should be speaking not just about the age of Aquarius, but of Aquarius-Leo. Leo is a fire sign whose qualities complement those of airy Aquarius. Thus along these lines we could see the Irvingite, Pentecostal and Carlylean interpretation of "he will baptize you with the Holy Spirit and with fire" as symbolising the change from the water and earth of Pisces-Virgo, to the air and fire of Aquarius-Leo.

The need to think in terms of pairs of opposites is not a peripheral matter and is the subject of much concern among astrologers today. As Sandra Levy says in *The Astrological Journal*, "Recently there has been a lot said and written about the emergence of long-suppressed Virgo as the opposite sign and feminine principle of the Piscean Age. The extremism of Women's Lib and materialistic science are said to be two examples of this".[19] She goes on to quote Liz Greene who says that as we move into the Aquarian age, it will only be by recognising Leo, the feminine principle, that we will be able "to heal the terrible split between the opposites which has occurred in the last age".[20] Aquarius must not become split off from Leo in the new age in the way Pisces separated from Virgo in the last. On this analogy we may say that we must be open to Christ's new baptism "with the Holy Spirit *and with fire*".

An Aquarian Exposition of the Day of Pentecost

Having looked at these two possible forerunners of Aquarian spirituality, let us now go back to *Acts 2* and examine the first 18 verses in closer detail. Let us see whether they fit an Aquarian interpretation.

> Verses 1-2: When the day of Pentecost had fully come, they were all together in one place. And suddenly a sound came from heaven like the rush of a mighty wind, and it filled all the house where they were sitting.

The Hebrew word *ruach* and its Greek equivalent *pneuma* can be translated either as "wind" or "spirit". The Spirit is of the air. It is in that sense Aquarian. The suddenness of its coming is like Uranus, the new ruler of Aquarius. As Alan Oken says, "Uranus acts suddenly. It is inconventional, forceful, and often violent in its manner of expression".[21]

> Verse 3: And there appeared to them tongues as of fire, distributed and resting on each one of them.

Here is the "and with fire" we have just discussed. It is the sign of spiritual refining and the element of Leo.

> Verse 4: And they were filled with the Holy Spirit and began to speak in tongues, as the Spirit gave them utterance.

The actual phenomenon of speaking in other tongues is complex and controversial. Many studies for and against Pentecostal and Charismatic experiences have been written in recent years.[22] What is significant for us is that this "unconventional" sign had a miraculous outcome: it enabled them all to understand each other's languages, as the story goes on to tell:

> Verses 5-8: Now there were dwelling in Jerusalem Jews, devout men from every nation under heaven. And at this sound the multitude came together, and they were bewildered, because each one heard them speaking in his own language. And they were amazed and wondered, saying, "Are not all these who are speaking Galileans? And how is it that we hear, each of us in his own native language?".

This experience of all understanding in their own languages is usually thought of as an empowerment of the disciples for mission[23] and as the symbolic reversal of the experience at Babel where "the Lord confused the language of all the earth" (*Genesis* 11:9).[24] But it could also fit an Aquarian interpretation, for the Aquarian glyph:♒is the sign of communication. Unity, co-operation and synthesis are also some of its attributes, as Vera Reid explains: "Its characteristics are unity, vision, memory, co-operation, synthesis . . . and through it the three aspects of mind – consciousness, unconsciousness and superconsciousness seek simultaneous expression".[25]

Verses 9-11: Parthians and Medes and Elamites and residents of Mesopotamia, Judea and Cappadocia, Pontus and Asia, Phrygia and Pamphylia, Egypt and the parts of Libya belonging to Cyrene, and visitors from Rome, both Jews and proselytes, Cretans and Arabians, we hear them telling in our own tongues the mighty works of God.

Scholars have often wondered why Luke chose such an odd list of countries to represent "every nation under heaven". Attempts have been made to find some symbolic order, most impressive of which, as J.W.Packer points out "is that based on astrological geography, whereby each country is allotted to one of the signs of the Zodiac".[26] He goes on to refer to the list drawn up by Paul of Alexandria in 378 A.D. This list, given in full by Ernst Haenchen, is "1. Aries = Persia. 2. Taurus = Babylon. 3. Gemini = Cappadocia. 4. Cancer = Armenia. 5. Leo = Asia. 6. Virgo = Hellas and Ionia. 7. Libra = Libya and Cyrene. 8. Scorpio = Italy. 9. Sagittarius = Cilicia and Crete. 10. Capricorn = Syria. 11. Aquarius = Egypt. 12. Pisces = Red Sea and Indian lands'.[27] Haenchen discusses this list at length, agreeing with Harnack, Wellhausen and others that "Judea" is a late addition.[28] Leaving that out, it will be seen that Luke is in substantial agreement with

Paul of Alexandria. Gilles Quispel makes this clear by setting out the comparative lists:[29]

Zodiac	Paul of Alexandria	Acts
1. Aries	Persia	Parthians, Medes, Elamites
2. Taurus	Babylon	Mesopotamia
3. Gemini	Cappadocia	Cappadocia
4. Cancer	Armenia	Pontus
5. Leo	Asia Minor	Asia Minor
6. Virgo	Hellas and Ionia	Phrygia and Pamphylia
7. Libra	Libya and Cyrene	Libya and Cyrene
8. Scorpio	Italy	Rome
9. Sagittarius	Cilicia and Crete	Cretanus
10. Capricorn	Syria	Judea
11. Aquarius	Egypt	Egypt
12. Pisces	Red Sea and India	Arabs

The list of countries then, like the twelve jewels in the foundation of New Jerusalem, indicates once again that there is far more astrological symbolism in the New Testament than is generally realised. This being so, it seems ever more reasonable to suppose that an Aquarian interpretation of *Acts* 2:1-18 is worthy of consideration, particularly as the universalism displayed there seems to be an Aquarian characteristic. Once again, Reid's description is remarkably apt: "The true Aquarian knows no exclusive ties of race, colour, creed or family. To him all men are brothers and to all alike he extends the hand of friendship and goodwill".[30]

Verses 12-13: And all were amazed and perplexed, saying to one another, "What does this mean?" But others mocking said, "They are filled with new wine".

The amazement, perplexity and shock that was experienced as some said "What does this mean?" and others "They are filled with new wine" continues to correspond to the comments which Oken makes about Uranus where he says this revolutionary and surprising planet "tends to overthrow preconceived or conventional notions with its directness, originality, and intuitive perspective".[31]

Verses 14-17a: But Peter, standing with the eleven, lifted up his voice and addressed them, "Men of Judea and all who dwell in Jerusalem, let this be known to you, and give ear to my words. For these men are not drunk, as you suppose, since it is only the third hour of the day; but this is what was spoken by the prophet Joel: 'And in the last days it shall be . . .'

Peter gets up, asks for a hearing and starts to explain. He says that they are not drunk because it is too early in the day. No, this is the fulfilment of Joel's prophecy concerning the last days. Actually, Joel did not say "in the last days", but only "afterward" or "after these things". Luke has changed the *meta tauta* of the Septuagint into *en tais eschatais hēmērais*. Why has he done this? Robert Maddox suggests that he wanted to convey "either that the consummation is imminent, for there are not many days to run before it comes, or else that the expected new age, the age when fulfilment of God's promises is actually experienced, has already arrived".[32] All of which begins to look like another instance where "in the last days" could be interpreted as "at the end of the age" in the terms which we have already examined.

Verse 17: 'And in the last days it shall be, God declares, that I will pour out my Spirit upon all flesh, and your sons and your daughters shall prophesy, and your young men shall see visions, and your old men shall dream dreams;

The Spirit is to be poured out "upon all flesh". It is universal. In terms reminiscent of Teilhard de Chardin, Oken describes the "water" which Aquarius pours out as "the stream of universal consciousness, inspiration and intuition". He goes on to say "Aquarius, therefore, distributes the riches of life through an understanding of the nature of humanity." [33] In other words he is very democratic. He distributes the riches of his inspiration among the sons and the daughters, the young and the old.

Verse 18: Yea, and on my menservants and my maidservants in those days I will pour out my Spirit; and they shall prophesy.

He even distributes the gifts of his out-poured Spirit onto the servants, both men and women. Surely not on the slaves – and especially not on the *women* slaves – how outrageous! How much more democratic – even Women's Lib – can you get? Well this is not surprising to the Aquarian, as Oken explains: "Uranus is called the bohemian of the solar system because its vibrations demand freedom of behaviour on the personal level and the liberation of thought and movement from authoritarian control."[34]

It seems strange, almost incongruous, that this Aquarian interpretation fits the story of Pentecost and Pentecostalism so well. This apparent incongruity stems from the fact that the Pentecostal and New Age movements view each other with deep suspicion. It is not too much to say that Pentecostals and Charismatics are liable to condemn New Agers as being of the devil while the latter often think the former are narrow and bigoted. This is most unfortunate because, as has been shown, they have much in common and may be seen as authentic movements of the Spirit. This at least is the view of Kenneth Cuming, who suggests that if there is any devil's work afoot, it is in the division between them:

At the moment, another great upsurge of the Spirit is on its way. Within the Church itself, the great Charismatic movement of the Ministry of Healing is gathering momentum on all sides as many rush to join its ranks; the Pentecostal movement is likewise permeating all branches of the Church, whether Roman Catholic, Anglican or United Reform, and is sweeping through the Americas and even behind the Iron

Curtain. Outside the Church, the concept of another New Age dawning is being readily accepted, and New Age teachings promoted widely. Both are the promptings of the Holy Spirit, which is no respecter of persons. The two lines of approach should not be regarded as mutually incompatible, but rather as complementary and not antagonistic. For the Charismatic and Pentecostal movements are the spiritual-emotional wing; and the new schools of philosophy, science and psychology represent the spiritual-intellectual wing. Both together are thus the Wings of the Holy Spirit, and both have their allotted function in the New Age movement. Only the Devil wants them to be a "house divided against itself".[35]

If we were to continue this exposition of *Acts* 2, we would find that this chapter is just as Aquarian at its end as at its beginning, for in verses 44 and 45 it says: "And all who believed were together and had all things in common; and they sold their possessions and goods and distributed them to all, as any had need." This description of communal living corresponds exactly to the Aquarian characteristics of unity, co-operation and synthesis, already mentioned. As Vera Reid says, to the Aquarian "all men are brothers and to all alike he extends the hand of friendship."

It could also be demonstrated that just as the Pentecostal experiences of *Acts* 2 are being reproduced on a massive scale in our time, so the Early Church's expression of unity and co-operation can also be found in many of the most significant movements of this century. In the Church, for example, we could point to the ecumenical movement with its World Council of Churches, to the huge proliferation of basic Christian communities and to the growing House-Church movement. In international affairs we could instance the United Nations Organisation, the European Economic Community and the Organisation of African Unity. At the political and social levels the various labour, socialist and co-operative movements stand out as obvious examples. Even the dark spectre of World Communism can be seen from this perspective as a distorted expression of the same drive.

All these major movements, and many more, exemplify Aquaraian attributes. They can also be seen as the varied successors of those who, having experienced the miracle of understanding each other "in his own native language", were led to have "all things in common". They can, in fact, be described as expressions of the Aquarian Spirit. As nations throughout the world strive towards democracy and unity; as churches experience community and overcome age-old divisions; as individual souls reject superannuated symbols and are baptised with fire and with the Holy Spirit, so we perceive the signs of a world Pentecost, an outpouring of the Spirit "upon all flesh", a planetary move towards the age of Aquarius.

CHAPTER 8

CHRIST: THE AQUARIAN LOGOS

We have spent the last chapter identifying Aquarian symbolism and attributes in the New Testament and in the modern world. Our findings have centred around the second chapter of Acts, which would appear to be one which has central importance for our time. This is very significant, because it takes us back to the cycles of seven in the Jewish festivals, discussed in chapter 3. After all, Pentecost – *pentekostē* in Greek – means "fiftieth" and was the name given to what in earlier times was called the feast of Weeks. This, as we noted then, was one of the two biblical festivals which had to be computed by counting seven times seven plus one. It seems extraordinary that, without any preconceived notion as to where our researches might lead, the hunt for Aquarius has landed us fairly and squarely back at one of the two festivals associated with the number 50 and at the only one literally called "Fiftieth".

This is even more remarkable when we realise that we could interpret Jubilee, the other festival associated with the number 50, in exactly the same way. For the cause of freedom, from Rousseau[1] to Martin Luther King,[2] from Wilberforce[3] to Liberation Theology,[4] has been just as important during the last two centuries as egalitarianism and undoubtedly bears as close a resemblance to the Jubilee injunctions to "proclaim liberty" and free the slaves (*Lev.* 25), as socialism does to the Pentecostal imperative to have "all things in common". This Jubilee emphasis on freedom also fits an Aquarian interpretation, for its ruling planet Uranus "demands freedom of behaviour on the personal level and liberation of thought and movement from authoritarian control".[5] It would seem as though Uranus is just as much for freedom as equality and unity. In fact, according to Alan Oken, it turns out to be the complete revolutionary:

> The influence of Uranus through its revolutionary rays was felt in the United States in 1776, in France in 1789 . . . When there was no great revolution of the masses, there was the Aquarian desire for unity and brotherhood ("Liberté, Fraternité, Egalité') . . . Uranus' urge for freedom is always seen coupled with the desire for unification to take place within a given structure (Saturn).[6]

The Comma as Metaphor for the Age Change

Why should it be that the principles associated with Pentecost and Jubilee should bear such striking similarities to those which have dominated our religious and political world more and more during the last two hundred years? Why is it that the truths associated with these two festivals appear to have the life-force of history in them for our time? Why is it that it is these two festivals, and no others, which are so closely connected with the number 50? Is the number 50, in this sense, important for the understanding of our time?

I believe the answer to all these questions can be found in an understanding of our times as the "age change", the tumultuous period on the cusp between the ages of Pisces and Aquarius. As we discovered in chapter 3, the number 50 in music is associated both with harmony and with harmonic imperfection. The discrepancy between 7 octaves and 12 fifths, the Pythagorean Comma, by analogy therefore speaks of both humankind's quest for the perfection of harmony and at the same time of the discord by which he finds himself surrounded. It is this paradoxical musical analogy which aptly describes this period of the "age change" from Pisces to Aquarius, because the former is associated with the discord of dualism and the latter with the concord of a holistic view of things. As Carl Jung says,

> If, as seems probable, the aeon of the fishes is ruled by the archetypal motif of the hostile brothers, then the approach of the next Platonic month, namely Aquarius, will constellate the problem of the union of opposites.[7]

Paradoxically, therefore, the Comma represents "the problem of the union of opposites" - the problem of overcoming dualism with harmony, of reconciling the hostile brothers. Liz Greene, in *Relating*, speaks of the dualism of the Piscean age as being not only inherent in the sign of the two fishes swimming in opposite directions but also in the hostility between Pisces and its polar opposite Virgo. We have touched on this in chapter 7 but must now go into it in greater detail:

> But the values embodied by Pisces and its opposite sign, Virgo, have been inimical to each other for the last two thousand years. This enmity is very similar to that experienced by an individual at war with his own shadow. The qualities embodied by Virgo were forcibly repressed during the Piscean age. In consequence, the highest value – that absolute love for and forgiveness of mankind of which Christ is the most significant symbol – has not been given balance and form by the realistic earthy consciouness of Virgo.[8]

She goes on to identify "the enormous implications in this terrible split in the collective unconscious of man in the Piscean era". It has been a time when Virgo, the symbol of Woman, has been "charged with the projection of the collective shadow", with darkness, the demonic, weakness and inferiority. The Holy Trinity has been seen as masculine "while woman, matter, earth, remains below, in the grip of the Lord of the World."[9]

In contrast she says that we are now approaching the new age in which this "terrible split" will be overcome. There will be the possibilty of a union of opposites, but only if the Aquarian consciousness does not repress or reject its polar opposite Leo, the way Pisces treated Virgo:

> We may see words leaking into common speech which show us how far the new values have progressed: in the Piscean age, one spoke of love, compassion, selflessness and sacrifice, while now we speak of group consciousness, energy, organisation and discovery. Aquarius, with all its nobility, will wipe out the individual if it runs rampant; Leo, if it is suppressed and erupts, is the dictator, the megalomaniac, the true figure of the antichrist, whose individuality is the supreme value. Somewhere between these two we must steer our course.[10]

It is now possible to see from what Liz Greene says, that, just as the experience and ethics of Pentecost and Jubilee offer us a model with which to interpret the history of the last two hundred years, so the spiritual truths symbolised by the Pythagorean Comma offer us a psychological way of analysing the age change from Pisces to Aquarius. The number 50, with all its musical and spiritual ambiguities, could therefore very well be the number that epitomises this time of transition from the dissonances of Piscean dualism to the consonances of the Aquarian union of opposites.

The time and effort we have expended in attempting to understand the Comma, may now be proving to have been well worthwhile if it is giving us such a complex and profound metaphor for the basic consciousness of our age. David Tame, speaking of the comma, told us earlier that "The cycle of twelve perfect fifths did not *close* and finish a cycle of seven octaves, but exceeded it, and thus, as it were, spiralled *upward*",[11] and Herbert Whone similarly said "the fifth overshooting the mark opens the door to an infinity of frequences".[12] This upward spiral, "this infinity of frequencies" is our analogy for the period of the cusp of the ages in which we now find ourselves. It is this very discrepancy which appears to be our hope, our freedom and our future. For it is only a Comma – not a full stop – an age change, not an apocalypse. It is the very instability that propels us forward, the off-balancing impulse that moves all things onwards. It is the upward spiral of the galaxies, of DNA, of phylotaxis, of all growth and movement. It seems as though it could indeed be identified with the very pulse of life which we explored in chapter 4. If this is the case then it would certainly explain the centrality of the Spirit in both Pentecost and Jubilee. It would also confirm Tame's staggering assertion, quoted in chapter 4, that "it is by the phenomenon of Pythagoras' Comma that the very nature of our lives within the realm of mortality is arranged".[13]

The Logos and Aquarian Spirituality

I believe we can find a close link between what we have just been saying about the harmonious union of opposites and an important New Testament understanding of who Jesus was, which so far we have only touched on and must now examine more fully. This is further emphasised by Liz Greene where she says:

> We now talk about archetypes and energy rather than gods; to Aquarius, everything is energy and operates according to natural laws, and these energies exist within as well as outside man. God, to Aquarius, is the intelligent principle by which these laws, both physical and psychic operate.[14]

If we amalgamate Greene's description of the Aquarian perception of God as "the intelligent principle" of natural laws, with Jung's "union of opposites", we get something remarkably similar to the ancient concept of the Logos, the Word, as defined by its originator, the Greek philosopher Heraclitus (535-475 BC.). George S. Hendry, in *Theology of Nature* explains:

Heraclitus was interested in the process of change itself, and he sought to discover the law or principle that governs it. He found it in the conflict of opposites which, despite their opposition, interact harmoniously, according to the regulation of a principle, which he called the Logos and invested with divine attributes.[15]

This original definition of the Logos is clearly very like Greene's and Jung's Aquarian understanding of God. This likeness becomes even more marked when we realise that Heraclitus invented the word 'harmony', *harmonia*, to explain what he meant by the balance of conflicting opposites brought about by the Logos.[16] The similarity between the two systems of thought is remarkable and appears to agree to a great extent with much that we have been discovering in the course of this enquiry, not only about the number 50 and the Pythagorean Comma, but also about the music of the spheres, the harmonic universe, the measures of Solomon's temple and the consonances of the cube of the New Jerusalem. It seems therefore that we may rightfully ascribe all these Aquarian and harmonious attributes to Jesus Christ himself because, according to the famous prologue to John's gospel, he was the incarnation of the Logos:[17]

In the beginning was the Word [*Logos*], and the Word [*Logos*] was with God, and the Word [*Logos*] was God. He was in the beginning with God; all things were made through him, and without him was not anything made that was made.

It is surprising how quickly we have moved from what perhaps might have appeared to be no more than astrological and musicological speculations, to the interpretation of this key New Testament text. For key text this was, at least in the Early Church, as the writings of the Fathers such as Justin Martyr, Irenaeus, Tertullian, Clement of Alexandria, Origen, Eusebius and many others show. Justin Martyr called Heraclitus "a Christian before Christ" on the strength of it.[18] Irenaeus saw Christ as the proportion or "measure of the Father"[19] and Eusebius went even further in his Christianising of *harmonia* in his *Demonstratio Evangelica*. The Logos, he said:

> . . . always continuously pervades the whole matter of the elements and of actual bodies; and, as being creator – word of God, stamps on it the principles (*logoi*) of the wisdom derived from Him. He impresses life on what is lifeless and form on what is in itself formless and indeterminate, reproducing in the qualities of the bodies, the values and the unembodied forms inherent in Him; He sets into all-wise and all-harmonious motion things that are on their own account lifeless and immobile – earth, water, fire, and air: He orders everything out of disorder, giving development and completion: with the actual power of deity and logos He all but forces all things: He pervades all things and grasps all things, yet contracts no injury from nor is sullied in himself.[20]

In the context of this study, this passage must be regarded as an extraordinarily accurate and comprehensive description of the cosmic Christ. Eusebius has stolen my lines! This is Christ the Creator, the Pantocrator, as Paul called him.[21] This is the Christ of cosmology. It also reads like a commentary on the other text with which we began, *Colossians* 1:15-17, where Paul speaks of Christ as "the first-born of all creation":

> He is the image of the invisible God, the first-born of all creation; for in him all things were created, in heaven and on earth, visible and invisible, whether thrones or dominions or principalities or authorities – all things were created through him and for him. He is before all things, and in him all things hold together.

Paul's description is very like Eusebius' "He pervades all things and grasps all things". It is also very like

129

Greene's where she says "God, to Aquarius, is the intelligent principle by which these laws, both physical and psychic operate".

If the Early Church Fathers gave such centrality to this definition of Christ, then why did it not continue to occupy a position of central importance? There were many reasons for this but broadly speaking scholars agree that the Logos concept proved to be too vague and imprecise to express the subtle distinctions of the complex christological debates of the 3rd and 4th centuries. It could mean too many things, it was tainted with too many gnostic associations and its universalism became increasingly suspect. G.L.Prestige says "the doctrine of the Logos, great as was its importance for theology, harboured deadly perils in its bosom",[22] and T.E.Pollard asserts "In the Arian and Marcellan controversies,the inadequacy of the Logos-concept,however it is to be interpreted, as the basis for Christian thinking about Jesus Christ, is revealed".[23] Maurice Wiles adds that compared with the graphic and personal notion of Christ as "the Son of the Father", the Logos was pale and abstract: "Logos was a scholar's term; it was not well fitted to meet the religious needs of ordinary folk".[24] To these reasons we may add that the holistic and inclusive concept of the Logos proved increasingly inimical to the rise of Piscean ecclesiastical dualism.

For all these reasons, from the second half of the third century onwards, the mind of the Church moved slowly but firmly away from the belief that the Logos could be in creation or in humankind, even to a small degree, in the same way as it was in Christ. Maurice Wiles speaks of this fateful development:

The attempt to frame a theology of the divine Christ in terms of the Logos of God was a failure, but it was a noble failure. It was never fiercely repudiated, not totally abandoned; but it did gradually lose the centre of the stage. Theology underwent a gradual change of emphasis rather than a sudden reversal of direction. Many of the ideas which it had suggested lived on in new settings. Some of these which were eventually lost, were lost to the detriment of the Church's thought and life. The idea of a link between the universal Logos incarnate in Christ and the fragmentary Logos present in every man, provides a dimension to Christian theology which has often been unhappily absent.[25]

As Wiles says, "the idea of a link between the universal Logos incarnate in Christ and the fragmentary Logos present in every man ... has often been unhappily absent". However, if we have been justified in seeing a close connection between this ancient concept and the new spiritual consciousness of Aquarius, this should change. We should expect to see a return to the belief that the Logos which was incarnate in Christ, is also to some degree present in all humanity and in all creation. We should also expect to find a resurgence of belief in the incarnate Logos himself, the cosmic Christ. And this is indeed what is beginning to happen all over the world in this generation. There is an awakening to a new awareness of the universality of Christ's presence and power. Horizons are being widened and vision is being extended. On the cusp of the ages, the Aquarian Logos is revealing the truths of the ancient wisdom. He is giving:

> ... true understanding of things as they are: a knowledge of the structure of the world and the operation of the elements; the beginning and the end of epochs and their middle course; the alternating solstices and changing seasons; the cycles of the years and the constellations.

> (*Wisdom of Solomon* 7:17-19, N.E.B.)

Through this revelation of the knowledge of the structure and cycles of the cosmos "as they are", he is leading us to a new awareness of the point our planet has reached in cosmic time. We are beginning to be able to read the ominous signs of our times not as the countdown to catastrophe but as the birth pangs of a new epoch of

131

creation. For, as Liz Greene reminds us, "Astrological ages appear to commence with great heaves and groans, like the birth of any new thing into the world, and they are accompanied by the death pangs of the old era which engendered them".[26]

This is a message of hope for a confused and frightened world. There is a long-term future for us to which we can and should commit ourselves. It involves the acceptance of change, the willingness to work for, not against, nature, and the ability to see things whole. In this transition period we must seek to align ourselves "with the set of the celestial tides"[27] so that the conflict of opposites may be overcome and the true harmony of Christ be established in all things.

APPENDIX: THE SACRED GEOMETRY OF NEW JERUSALEM

To supplement our examination of St John's vision of the New Jerusalem, a geometric figure might be constructed to help in the process of changing the picture of the holy city from a heavenly metropolis to an image of the cosmos, as already described. One picture is worth a thousand words and a change of model can help us see the whole thing in a completely new way.

I propose drawing a model of the New Jerusalem according to the principles of sacred geometry.[1] Sacred geometry, as Robert Lawlor defines it in *Sacred Geometry, Philosophy and Practice*, was the ancient art-science of laying bare in two dimensions the underlying structure of the universe. Only straight-edge and compasses were allowed, and each number, ratio and shape corresponded to a spiritual reality or archetype according to the principle of correspondence which, simply stated, is: "as above, so below"; or "as in the macrocosm, so in the microcosm".[2]

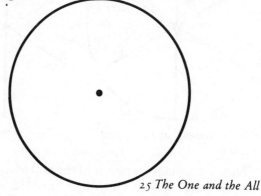

25 *The One and the All*

133

The Inner Circle

We start with a dot or point representing the One, that is, God as microcosm. Round it we draw a circle representing the All, that is God as macrocosm. As Hermes Trismegistus is reputed to have said: "God is a circle whose centre is everywhere and circumference is nowhere"[3] Keeping our compasses at the same span, we mark off the circumference of the circle into six equal portions, the first mark being at the top or bottom. Then we join these six points to the centre. This figure in its vertical line now represents the *axis mundi* or axle of the world round which the ancients believed the universe revolved. It also stands for the tree of life in the garden of Eden and in the New Jerusalem. The diagonal lines which intersect it represent the four rivers of Eden and the river of the water of life in the New Jerusalem. Altogether these six lines symbolise the cross of Christ and the *Chi-Rho* or *labarum* of the Constantinian Church, that is, the first two letters of Christ's name in Greek.[4]

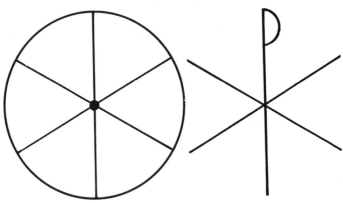

26 *The axis-mundi and the rivers of Eden*

27 *The* Chi-rho

Now we join up the points of the axes where they touch the circumference, thus making a six-sided hexagon. This hexagon is the same as a cube when seen at an angle of 45° with the foremost point and the rearmost point coinciding in the centre. This cube-as-hexagon is a most important figure and can easily be seen to be a model of the cube of the New Jerusalem. Remembering our key texts from St Paul, let us picture Jesus Christ as the central point of the circle where all the lines meet. This is him on his "throne" with his Father, the one in whom "all things hold together" (*Colossians* 1:17). St John says "I saw no temple in the city, for its temple is the Lord God Almighty and the Lamb" (*Revelation* 21:22). We can see from this simple geometric figure how Christ can be pictured as Saviour, in the cross and in the *Chi-Rho*, and as Creator in the central point which holds all things together. This is most important. Nothing that I say is designed to undermine the gospel of Christ as Saviour. But I do wish to see him as Creator in a way that does equal justice to his twofold function, for unless the Saviour can also be seen as the Creator, we shall remain trapped within the dualism which has separated Christians from creation and contributed so much to our present ecological impasse.

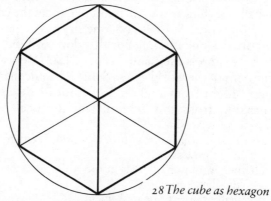

28 *The cube as hexagon*

From this figure we can see how Christ as both Creator and Saviour becomes, geometrically, the temple himself.

He literally *is* the temple! St John says he saw no temple in the city "for its temple is the Lord God the Almighty and the Lamb". Christ is the temple with his Father-God. This links up with his speaking of "the temple of his body" (*John 2:19*). It also links up with all those who are "in Christ", for St Paul says, "Do you not know that you are God's temple" (*1 Cor.* 3:16) and "Do you not know that your body is a temple of the Holy Spirit" (*1 Cor.* 6:19)? We may therefore also take this cube-as-hexagon to represent the Church, not so much as an organisation or building but more as a spiritual and physical relationship between Christ and the members of his body. For he is not only the "first-born of all creation", he is also the "head of the body, the church", as St Paul says in the sequel to our key text (*Col.* 1:18-20):

> He is head of the body, the church; he is the beginning, the first-born from the dead, that in everything he might be pre-eminent. For in him all the fullness of God was pleased to dwell, and through him to reconcile to himself all things, whether in earth or in heaven, making peace by the blood of his cross.

This way of looking at the person and work of Christ has a close affinity with the tradition of mystical thought which sees him as the still point of light at the centre of the turning world. St John says "the city has no need of sun or moon to shine upon it, for the glory of God is its light, and its lamp is the Lamb" (*Rev.* 21:23). Jesus said "I am the light of the world' (*John* 8:12). The Nicene Creed calls him "Light from Light". T.S. Eliot in *Burnt Norton* is speaking from this biblical and mystical background when he writes:

> At the still point of the turning world. Neither flesh
> nor fleshless;
> Neither from nor towards at the still point, there
> the dance is,
> But neither arrest nor movement . . .
> Except for the point, the still point,
> There would be no dance, and there is only the dance.[5]

The Intermediate Circles

Let us now move on to the next stage in the construction of our model. With compasses still at the length of the radius of the circle, from each of the points where the axes touch the circumference, describe segments of arcs furthest away from the centre of the circle. Then extend each of the axes outwards until they cross these arcs. With these intersection points as the centres, describe six circles round the central circle. You will find that, drawn accurately, these six circles touch the central circle and each other tangentially.

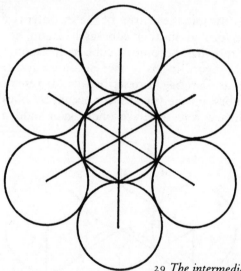

29 *The intermediate circles*

You have now drawn a picture of the beginning of all creation when God created everything in six days and rested on the seventh (*Gen.* 1 – 2:3). These six circles also symbolise the six days of the working week surrounding the sabbath. Could they perhaps also be "the seven spirits who are before his throne" (*Rev.* 1:4) or "the seven angels who had the seven bowls full of the seven last plagues" (*Rev.* 21:9)?

These seven circles also represent the solar system with the Sun at the centre and the Moon, Mars, Mercury, Jupiter, Venus and Saturn round about. These were the seven planets of ancient astronomy which are still associated with the seven days of the week, namely: Sunday = Sun's-day, Monday = Moon's-day, Tuesday = Mars'-day (mardi), Wednesday = Mercury's-day (mercredi, Wodensday), Thursday = Jupiter's-day (jeudi, Thorsday), Friday = Venus'-day (vendredi, Friasday), Saturday = Saturn's-day. For clarity of derivation I have put in the French and Norse equivalents.

If you now join the centres of the six outer circles, you will have formed another cube-as-hexagon, so that the whole figure has become a cube-as-hexagon within a cube-as-hexagon. It has in fact become a hypercube or tesseract, as Carl Sagan described it: "It resembles two nested cubes, all the vertices connected by lines". In an extraordinary way we have once again suddenly leapt

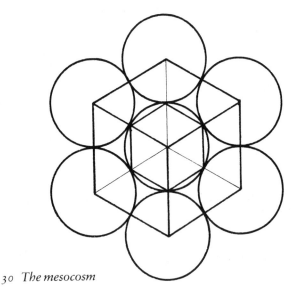

30 *The mesocosm*

138

from what we thought was purely an ancient way of picturing the cosmos, to contemporary astro-physics. If we now allow ourselves to return to the *Sefer Yesira*, the *Book of Creation*, we can see how our model can also be further developed to express the "Twelve edges of a cube" which "expand continually for ever and ever".

The Outer Circles

The ideas of the expanding universe, the nested cubes of the tesseract, the cube of the cosmos and the New Jerusalem as cosmic model, all come together in this geometric figure and can be even further elucidated if we enlarge it yet again. On the same principle as before, extend the six axes until they cross the segments of arcs formed by the circumferences of circles whose centres are the points at which these axes cross the outer circumference of the six circles. At these intersections describe six circles all of the same radii as the others. Join the centres of these six outer circles and describe equal circles in the six gaps between them by the same means. You now have a cube-as-hexagon within a cube-as-hexagon within a cube-as-hexagon. These are the microcosm, the meso-cosm (intermediate) and the macrocosm. The macrocos-mic cube represents the universe expanding for ever and ever and the twelve outer circles represent the twelve divisions of the heavens, the constellations of the zodiac, the foundations of the New Jerusalem "adorned with every jewel". They also symbolise "the names of the twelve tribes of the sons of Israel" (*Rev.* 21:12) and "the twelve names of the twelve apostles of the Lamb" (*Rev.* 21:14).

We have now completed the sacred geometry of the New Jerusalem as a "representation of the cosmos" and a "replica of the universe". It offers a simple yet profound picture which may help us to think holistically about Jesus Christ as the one through whom all things were made (*John* 1:3). It would also appear to unite the

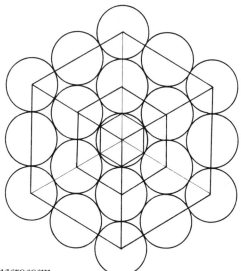

31 The macrocosm

container, extensive and geometric concepts of space which have been at the centre of controversy in theoretical physics for the last three hundred years.

Solomon's Seal

Before we finish this particular exercise I would like to mention one more geometric symbol. If we return to the elements of our paradigm, that is, to the central circle with the six circles round it, and if we remove all traces of the cube-as-hexagon, and then join the centres of the first, third and fifth circles and the centres of the second, fourth and sixth, we have described two intersecting equilateral triangles. If we then remove the circles, we are left with only these two triangles. This figure is the six-pointed star known as Solomon's Seal, a most important geometric construction, as J.C. Cooper explains:

The double triangle, the six-pointed star, the Seal of Solomon, the Mogun David, indicates that 'every true analogy must be applied universally', 'as above so below'; it is the union of opposites, male and female, positive and

140

negative; fire and water; evolution and involution; inter-
penetration, each being the image of the other; the perfect
balance of complementary forces . . . As the Seal of Solomon
it is also the figure of the Preserver and gives spirit power
over matter.[6]

32 *Solomon's Seal*   33 *The T'ai Chi*

In other words it is the biblical equivalent of the Chinese
symbol of the yin-yang balance, the *T'ai Chi*.

The *T'ai Chi* or *Ta ki* has become very well-known in
recent years because of the influence of Taoist philosophy
in the West particularly through such books as *The Tao of
Physics* and *The Turning Point* by Fritjof Capra. Like
Solomon's Seal, it symbolises the union of opposites held
together in harmonious balance, interpenetrating and
interdependent, each containing the germ of the other in
perpetual alternation.

All the meanings of Solomon's Seal listed by Cooper
complement those which we have already drawn out of
our own geometric model, to a remarkable degree. It is
also extraordinary that, as with the cubic universe and the
tesseract, recent advances in electron microscopy reveal
how similar the structure of Solomon's Seal is to the basic
structure of crystal. Professor Gareth Thomas of the
University of California has demonstrated, using conver-

CHRIST AND THE COSMOS

gent beam microscopy, that if a sharply focused beam of electrons moving at over half the speed of light is bounced off a silicon crystal, an image is formed (a zone axis

34 *Zone axis pattern of a silicon crystal (Professor Gareth Thomas)*

pattern) of a complex geometric structure at the heart of which are two equilateral triangles intersecting in the form of Solomon's Seal. At the centre of this is a luminous dot.[7] If we remember to what extent the silicon chip is responsible for our present communications revolution, we shall come nearer to realising that in sacred geometry and these biblical texts, we are encountering fundamental truths which are just as relevant today as they ever were. Modern science is stumbling upon this ancient wisdom in spite of its desire to be exclusively materialistic – to be concerned only with knowledge, not wisdom. Perhaps by bringing these two disciplines together, the old and the new, a union of opposites, a "perfect balance of complementary forces" could be achieved.

But the final question must be: why is Solomon's Seal, or the Star of David as it is popularly called, still the symbol of the Jews? Why is it that this six-pointed star is seen flying on every Israeli national flag? Could one answer be that the link between the Bible and sacred geometry is very strong – so strong that those who believed in the scriptures saw the geometric symbol of the union of opposites as the perfect expression of their faith? If this is so then we can only lament the extent to which that link has been broken and that wisdom lost.

It is becoming increasingly clear that what we are dealing with in this field is not something which is peripheral to the Bible. It is not eccentric or marginal. It is a lost tradition which comes as much from the heart of the scriptures as the forgotten truths about the cosmic Christ.

ENDNOTES

CHAPTER 1

1 "The White Train", *The Observer Colour Supplement*, London 7 October, 1984.

2 It is ironical that the Greek word *apokalupsis* simply means "unveiling" and hence "revelation". It is a sad reflection on Christian usage that it has come to have its negative "apocalyptic" meaning.

3 John F.Walvoord, *The Revelation of Jesus Christ*, Marshall, Morgan and Scott, London 1966, p323: "It also could be in the form of a pyramid with sides sloping to a peak at the height indicated . . . This would have certain advantages . . . because this shape provides a vehicle for the river of life to proceed out of the throne of God, which seems to be at the top, to find its way to the bottom, assuming our experience of gravity will be somewhat normal also in the new earth". See also W.H. Simcox, *The Revelation*, Cambridge University Press, 1902, p136 for similar practical considerations!

4 See F.F. Bruce, *A New Testament Commentary*, Pickering & Inglis, London and Glasgow 1969, p664.

5 *Sibylline Oracles* V, line 251 (88 – 130 A.D.).

6 eg. Henry Barclay Swete, *The Apocalypse of St John*, Macmillan, London 1907, p289; Martin Kiddle, *The Revelation of St John*, Hodder and Stoughton, London 1940, p430.

7 Lewis Mumford, *The City in History*, Secker and Warburg, London 1961, p31. For a detailed expression of Mumford's position, with special reference to ancient Mesopotamia, see Thorkild Jacobson (with Frankfort and others)*Before Philosophy*, Pelican/Penguin 1971 edn., chapter 5, "Mesopotamia: the cosmos as a state".

8 Lewis Mumford,*op. cit.* p49.

9 eg. Philip Carrington, *The Meaning of the Revelation*,

144

S.P.C.K., London 1931, p346; Austin Farrar, *The Revelation of St John the Divine*, Clarendon, Oxford 1964, p218; Edward Schick, *The Revelation of St John*, Sheed and Ward, London, Vol 2, p105; Thomas Kelper, *The Book of Revelation*, Oxford University Press 1957, p213.

10   eg. Isbon T. Beckwith, *The Apocalypse of John*, Baker Book House, Grand Rapids, 1967 edn., p760; G.E. Ladd, *A Commentary on the Revelation of John*, Eerdmans 1972, p282.

11   M.R. Newbolt, *The Book of Unveiling*, S.P.C.K. London 1952, p197.

12   Otto Neugebauer, *The Exact Sciences in Antiquity*, Dover, New York 1969, pp93 and 36 respectively.

13   Plato, *Timaeus*, section 22.

14   Plato, *op. cit.* section 23.

15   Plato, *op. cit.* section 22.

16   György Doczi, *The Power of Limits: proportional harmonies in nature, art and architecture*, Shambhala, Boulder, London 1981.

17   *Sefer Yesira*, paragraph 47. See Peter Hayman "Some observations on Sefer Yesira (1). Its Use of Scripture", *Journal of Jewish Studies* Vol XXXV No. 2, Autumn 1984, Oxford p176. Hayman's observations are based on Professor I. Gruenwald's "Preliminary Critical Edition of Sefer Yesira", *Israel Oriental Studies*, I, 1971, p163. Gruenwald's edition is of the hitherto neglected long recension in the oldest extant manuscript of the book: *Vatican (Cat. Assemani)* 299 (8), fols 66a – 71b. Some scholars argue a later date for this document.

18   Carl Sagan, *Cosmos*, Book Club Associates, London, 1980, p264.

19   For exceptions to this see G.R. Beasley-Murray, *Revelation*, Marshal, Morgan and Scott, London 1974, p325n.

20   Athanasius Kircher, *Oedipus Aegyptiacus*, II, ii 177 ff, 1653.

21   R.H. Charles, *The Revelation of St John*, T. and T. Clark Edinburgh 1920, Vol 2, p167.

22   eg. Martin Kiddle, *op. cit.* p434.

23   eg. Ronald H. Preston and Anthony Hanson, *The

Revelation of St John the Divine, S.C.M. London 1973, p132; G.B. Caird, *The Revelation of St John the Divine*, Black, London 1966, p277.

24   Leon Morris, *The Revelation of St John*, Tyndale, London 1969, p252.

25   G.R. Beasley-Murray, *op. cit.* p325.

26   G.R. Beasley-Murray, *op. cit.* p323.

27   Austin Farrar, *A Rebirth of Images*, Dacre, London 1949, p216.

28   J. Massyngberde Ford, *Revelation*, Doubleday, New York 1975, p343.

29   J.C. Cooper, *An Illustrated Encyclopaedia of Traditional Symbols*, Thames and Hudson 1978, p198.

30   R.H. Charles, *op. cit.* p170.

31   Rabbi Johanan, *Sanhedrin* 100a and Baba bathra 75; eg. H.B. Swete, *op. cit.* p294; M. Kiddle, *op. cit.* p435; L. Morris, *op. cit.* p253.

32   R.H. Charles, *The Apocrypha and Pseudepigraphia of the Old Testament*, Clarendon, Oxford 1913, Vol II, p237.

33   Willaim Barclay, *The Revelation of St John*, St Andrew Press, Edinburgh, second 1976 edn., Vol 2, p214.

34   J.C. Cooper, *op. cit.* p128.

35   G.R. Beasley-Murray, *op. cit.* p326.

36   William Barclay, *op. cit.* p214.

37   eg. the sixteenth-century paraphrase of St Augustine's hymn "Jerusalem, my Happy Home", *The English Hymnal*, No. 638:

> Thy turrets and thy pinnacles
>   With carbuncles do shine;
> Thy very streets are paved with gold,
>   Surpassing clear and fine;
>
> Thy houses are of ivory,
>   Thy windows crystal clear;
> Thy tiles are made of beaten gold –
>   O God that I were there!

See also St Bernard's "Jerusalem the Golden", *The English Hymnal* 412 for "halls of Zion" and Samuel Johnson's "City of God", *The English Hymnal* 375, for watch-fires gleaming and towers arising.

38   *plateia* could possibly be generic for 'streets' as in *Rev.*
     11:8; cf G.B.Caird *op. cit.* p278.

39   eg Charles A. Sorrell and George F. Sandstrom, *The
     Rocks and Minerals of the World*, Collins, London 1982
     edn., p38 "Crystal Systems : Cubic Systems".

40   Mellie Uyldert, *The Magic of Precious Stones*, Turnstone,
     Wellingborough, 1981.

41   Ra Bonewitz, *Cosmic Crystals*, The hidden world of
     crystals and the New Age application of crystal energies.
     Turnstone, Wellingborough 1984, p10.

42   Francis Hitching, *The World Atlas of Mysteries*, Pan,
     London 1979, pp56, 57.

43   Plato, *Phaedo*, sections 109a – 110d.

44   Ra Bonewitz, *op. cit.* p130.

CHAPTER 2

1   Leon Morris, *The Revelation of St John*, Tyndale,
    London 1969, p250.

2   T.F. Glasson, *The Revelation of St John*, Cambridge
    University Press 1969, p118.

3   Nigel Pennick, *Sacred Geometry*, Turnstone, Welling-
    borough 1980, p60.

4   Nigel Pennick, *op. cit.* p118.

5   Percy Scholes, *The Concise Oxford Dictionary of Music*,
    London, Oxford University Press 1973 edn., p5.

6   Guy Murchie, *Music of the Spheres*, Rider/Hutchinson,
    London 1961, p362.

7   The extent to which these terms were part of the
    vocabulary of the early Church is shown, for instance, in
    Tatians' "Harmony of the Four Gospels" known as the
    Diatessaron.

8   For a general introduction to classical architecture as
    frozen music see Claude Bragdon, *The Beautiful Necess-
    ity, Architecture as "Frozen Music"*, Quest Books,
    London 1978 edn.

9   C.F. Burney, *The Books of Kings*, Clarendon, Oxford
    1903, p77.

10 James A. Montgomery, *The Books of Kings*, T. and T. Clark, Edinburgh 1951, p158.

11 John Gray, *I and II Kings*, S.C.M. London 1964, p173.

12 James A. Montgomery, *op. cit.* p152: "The shrine of the sanctuary is a cube of 20 cubits; for such proportion cf. the Meccan Ka'ba (ie.'dice cube'), which is 12 × 12m square, 15m high". This is hardly relevant let alone illuminating but better than all the rest who are more concerned with the gold-plating.

13 J.C. Cooper, *An Illustrated Encyclopaedia of Traditional Symbols*, Thames and Hudson, London 1978, p116.

14 Robert Lawlor, *Sacred Geometry*, Thames and Hudson, London 1982, p58.

15 See *Enclyclopaedia Judaica*, Jerusalem 1971, Vol 7, p379 for full explanation of gematria viz: "It consists of explaining a word or group of words according to the numerical value of the letters . . ." etc.; "The use of letters to signify numbers . . ." etc. It was practised widely throughout the ancient world. Thus in Greek *alpha* = 1, *beta* = 2 and in Hebrew *aleph* = 1, *beth* = 2 etc.

16 John Michell, *City of Revelation*, Abacus, London 1973, pp74-75.

17 eg. Alfred Edersheim, *The Temple, Its Ministry and Services*, Eerdmans, Grand Rapids 1978 edn., pp186-87.

18 Roger Cook,*The Tree of Life*, Thames and Hudson, Avon, London, New York, 1974, p119: "The sap of the tree becomes the precious 'oil of life' that burns in fruit and flower". cf S.T.Coleridge's description of paradise as an oriental idyll "Where blossomed many an incense-bearing tree". For an excellent discussion of Eden in relation to Xanadu, see E.S. Shaffer, *Kubla Khan and the Fall of Jerusalem*, Cambridge University Press 1975, pp96 ff.

19 J. Robinson, *The First Book of Kings*, Cambridge University Press1972, p81: "This custom was in origin a cereal offering".

20 Roger Cook, *op. cit.* p119: "In Judaism, the Tree of Life is most often represented by the flowering almond tree, the tree which, in the Near East, heralds and hastens the spring, its radiant white blossoms appearing long before

its leaves". See also L.Yardin, *The Tree of Light*, Horovitz, London 1971, p40.

21 *Encyclopaedia Judaica*, Vol 15. p950

22 John Gray, *op. cit.* p171.

23 *ibid.*

24 J.C. Cooper, *op. cit.* p125: "Palm; *Arabian*: the Tree of Life".

25 C.F.D. Moule, *The Origin of Christology*, Cambridge University Press 1977, p90.

26 John Bowker, *Jesus and the Pharisees*, Cambridge University Press1973, p49.

27 eg. Jacob at Bethel, *Gen.* 28:16-17 and Solomon's dedicatory prayer 1 *Kings* 8:27.

28 F.F. Bruce, *The Acts of the Apostles*, Tyndale, London 1951, p177.

29 Bertil Gärtner, *The Areaopagus Speech and Natural Revelation*, Gleerup, Uppsala 1955, p251. He concludes that the passage is Pauline and that other references indicate that the Gentiles have not lacked testimony to God as "the God Who is the Creator and Preserver of the created world".

CHAPTER 3

1 Maurice Farbridge, *Studies in Biblical and Semitic Symbolism*, Ktav. Inc. New York 1970, p119.

2 Ethelbert W. Bullinger, *Number in Scripture*, Eyre and Spottiswoode, London 1894, p158.

3 G.A.F. Knight, *Leviticus*, St Andrew Press, Edinburgh 1981, p152:"Seven is the holy number".

4 J.R. Porter, *Leviticus*, Cambridge University Press 1976, p38: "Seven appears as a sacred number in the Old Testament and also throughout the ancient Near East".

5 Ethelbert Bullinger, *ibid.* who calls seven "the great number in *spiritual perfection*".

6 Maurice Farbridge, *op. cit.* p135.

7 Maurice Farbridge, *ibid.*

8 Maurice Farbridge, *ibid.*

9   J.C. Cooper, *An Illustrated Encyclopaedia of Traditional Symbols*, Thames and Hudson, London 1978, pp106-107.

10   See John Michell, *City of Revelation*, Abacus, London 1973, p65: "the number seven is rarely apparent in physical nature, corresponding rather to the spiritual forces that regulate the cycles of time and human development".

11   See Ernest McClain, *The Myth of Invariance*, Shambhala, Boulder 1978, chapter 10 "Babylon and Sumer", section on sexagesimal arithmetic, pp131-141.

12   For a detailed comparison between Leviticus and earlier calendars, especially Deuteronomy 16, see Martin Noth, *Leviticus*, S.C.M. 1965, pp165-176.

13   Scholars have been divided as to what the literal Hebrew "from the morrow of the sabbath" means. For a summary of traditional opinions see N.H. Snaith, *Leviticus and Numbers*, Nelson, London 1967, p153.

14   N.H. Snaith, *op. cit.* p155, points out that this was also "the ecclesiastical New Year, since in pre-exilic times the new year began with the autumn festival".

15   N.H. Snaith, *op. cit.* p163.

16   For a graphic and ecological summary of Tabernacles see G.A.F. Knight, *op. cit.* p144-145.

17   Scholars are divided on whether the Jubilee was the forty-ninth or the fiftieth year. For a full discussion of the views of L.B. Paton, H. Strack, J. and H. Lewy, E. Stone, E.R. Leach, Zeitlin, Klostermann, North, Kugler and others, see Donald Wilford Blosser, *Jesus and the Jubilee*, unpublished Ph.D. thesis, St Andrews University, St Mary's College Library 1979, pp13-17.

18   Alfred Sendrey, *Music in Ancient Israel*, Vision, London 1969, p371.

19   J.R. Porter, *op. cit.* p184. cf G.A.F. Knight *op. cit.* p152: "The figures seven times seven thus represent the ultimate in holiness".

20   Robert Graves, *The White Goddess*, Faber and Faber, London 1961, chapter 15 "The Seven Pillars" pp259-271. See also Desmond Varley, *Seven: the Number of Creation*, G. Bell, London 1976, pp1-28.

21 Geoffrey Ashe, *The Ancient Wisdom*, Abacus, London 1977, pp120-126.

22 For a wealth of comparative material on this theme see Richard J. Clifford, *The Cosmic Mountain in Canaan and the Old Testament*, Harvard University Press, Cambridge Mass. 1972.

23 Percy Scholes, *The Oxford Companion to Music*, Oxford University Press London p591. He describes the monochord as "nothing but a sound-box over which is stretched a single string which can be divided at any point by a movable bridge, the position of which can be accurately determined by a scale of measurements marked on the surface over which it moves. The ratios of intervals and many others of the facts that make up the foundations of the science of acoustics were discovered by its use, and for five thousand years it gave rise to intricate mathematical calculations".

24 Robert K.G. Temple, *The Sirius Mystery*, Sidgwick and Jackson, London 1976, pp189-190, relates the Jubilee cycle to the orbit of the star Sirius B. He argues that because Moses wrote Leviticus and was "an initiate of Egypt", the 50-year cycle originated with the pre-dynastic Egyptians (the Dogons). Commenting on his belief that the Jubilee year was never kept, he says "Obviously the Hebrews did not understand the fifty-year orbit of Sirius B which Moses . . . presumably had in mind". I believe he is stretching the evidence considerably here, which is neither obvious nor presumable.

25 Herbert Whone, *The Hidden Face of Music*, Gollancz, London 1974 pp56-57.

26 Jack Finegan, *Handbook of Biblical Chronology*, Princeton University Press 1964, pp35-36.

27 Jack Finegan, *op. cit.* p37.

28 Ernest McClain, *op. cit.* p96.

29 Alain Daniélou, *Introduction to the Study of Musical Scales*, The India Society, London 1943, pp70-71.

30 David Tame, *The Secret Power of Music*, Turnstone, Wellingborough 1984, p249.

31 David Tame, *op. cit.* p250.

32 David Tame, *op. cit.* p38.

33   See N.H. Snaith, *op. cit.* p156.

CHAPTER 4

1   eg. Burton Scott Eastern, *The Gospel According to St Luke*, T. and T. Clark, Edinburgh 1926, p156, who says that the seventy merely helped Christ "to make the most of a short visit"; H. Balmforth, *The Gospel According to St Luke*, Clarendon, Oxford 1930, p200; Norval Geldenhuys, *Commentary on the Gospel of Luke*, Marshall, Morgan and Scott, London 1950, p299, who says they were appointed solely "to bring spiritual ministration and prepare His way in the towns and villages that he still wishes to visit during the few months before His crucifixion".

2   eg. Alfred Plummer, *The Gospel According to St Luke*, T. and T. Clark, Edinburgh 1905, p269; W. Manson, *The Gospel of Luke*, Hodder and Stoughton, London 1930, p123; William Arndt, *The Gospel According to St Luke*, Concordia, St Louis 1956, p280; W. R. F. Browning, *The Gospel According to St Luke*, S.C.M. London 1960, p109; D.W.Cleverly Ford, *A Reading of St Luke's Gospel*, Hodder and Stoughton, London 1967, p139.

3   eg. Alfred Plummer, *ibid*; W.R.F.Browning, *ibid.*

4   E. Earle Ellis, *The Gospel of Luke*, Nelson, London 1966, pp153-154.

5   G.H.P.Thompson, *The Gospel According to Luke*, Oxford University Press 1972, p159.

6   John Martin Creed, *The Gospel According to St Luke*, Macmillan, London 1930, p144.

7   E.J. Tinsley, *The Gospel According to Luke*, Cambridge UniversityPress 1965, p113.

8   Bruce M. Metzger, *Historical and Literary Studies*, E. J. Brill, Leiden 1968, chapter 7 "Seventy or Seventy-Two Disciples?", p76.

9   Bruce M. Metzger, *A Textual Commentary on the Greek New Testament*, United Bible Societies, London 1975, p151, paragraphs in square brackets by Kurt Aland.

10   I. Howard Marshall, *The Gospel of Luke*, Paternoster, Exeter 1978, p415.

11   *Encyclopaedia Judaica*, Jerusalem 1971, Vol 4, p852.

12   Giorgio de Santillana and Hertha von Dechend, *Hamlet's Mill*, Gambit, Ipswich 1969, p66: "Hipparchus in 127 B.C. called it the Precession of the Equinoxes. There is good reason to assume that he actually rediscovered this, that it had been known some thousand years previously, and that on it the Archaic Year based its long-range computation of time".

13   *Everyman's Encyclopaedia*, Dent, London 3rd edn. 1949, Vol 10, p630.

14   Giorgio de Santillana and Hertha von Dechend, *op. cit.* p59.

15   Rodney Collin, *The Theory of Celestial Influence*, Vincent Stuart, London 1954, p245.

16   William Stirling, *The Canon*, Garnstone, London 1974, p101.

17   Guy Lyon Playfair and Scott Hill, *The Cycles of Heaven*, Pan, London 1979, p197.

18   Ernest McClain, *The Myth of Invariance*, Shambala, Boulder 1978, p100.

19   Alain Daniélou, *Introduction to the Study of Musical Scales*, London 1943, p68.

20   David Tame, *The Secret Power of Music*, Turnstone, Wellingborough 1984, p249.

21   David Tame, *op. cit.* p22.

22   David Tame, *op. cit.* p23.

23   Gerhard von Rad, *Genesis*, S.C.M., London 1961, p47.

24   H. C. Leupold, *Exposition of Genesis*, Evangelical Press, London 1942, p48.

25   H. C. Leupold, *op. cit.* p50.

26   David Tame, *op. cit.* pp232-233.

27   Ernest McClain, *op. cit.* p124, re Rabbi Schochet.

28   Ernest McClain, *op. cit.* pp124-127.

29   David Tame, *op. cit.* p22: "Inaudible to the human ear, this Cosmic Vibration was the origin and basis of all the matter and energy in the universe. In its purest, least differentiated form, this Cosmic Sound was known to the Hindus as OM".

30   Captain Bruce Cathie, *The Pulse of the Universe: Harmonic 288*, Reed, London 1977, flyleaf.

31 David Tame, *op. cit.* p249.

32 Douglas Adams, *The Hitch-hiker's Guide to the Galaxy*, Pan, London 1979, pp134-136.

33 Strangely enough the numbers 5 and 72 also link us to the variant tradition which said that the Septuagint was translated by 72 scholars *and by five*. Henry G. Meecham, *The Oldest Version of the Bible*, Holborn, London 1932, p172, says "One tradition assigns the work of *transliteration* to five men, the *translation* to seventy-two men, each company carrying out its task in the time of Ptolemos". Carl Clemen, *Primitve Christianity and its Non-Jewish Sources*, T. andT. Clark, Edinburgh 1912, p103, suggests that "the seventy-two and the five were still felt to be component parts of the year of three hundred and sixty days".

CHAPTER 5

1 Gerhard Kittel, (ed.), *Theological Dictionary of the New Testament*, Eerdmans, Grand Rapids 1964, Vol 1, pp 198-209.

2 Gerhard Kittel, *op. cit.* p204.

3 Don Cupitt, *The Sea of Faith*, B.B.C, London 1984, p106. For a summary of this school of "consistent eschatology" see chapter 4 "Going by the Book".

4 Albert Nolan, *Jesus Before Christianity, The Gospel of Liberation*, Darton, Longman and Todd, London 1977, p18.

5 Albert Nolan, *op. cit.* p90.

6 D. S. Russell, *The Jews from Alexander to Herod*, Oxford University Press 1967, p140.

7 D. S. Russell, *ibid.*

8 D. S. Russell, *op. cit.* p141.

9 It is interesting to note that R. H. Charles says in *The Book of Jubilees*, Black, London 1902, p37, that Jubilees 4:17, mentioned by Russell, "refers mainly to 1 Enoch lxxii – lxxxii". This is "The Book of the Courses of the Heavenly Luminaries" in which we found justification for suggesting that the gates of New Jerusalem were "the

portals of heaven", in chapter 1. Howard Clark Kee says that this aspect of Enochic literature "was probably influenced by Babylonian astrology, in that it lays stress on the movement of the celestial order and the divinely intended earthly order". *The Origins of Christianity*, S.P.C.K., London 1980, p181.

10   C. G. Jung, *Aion*, Princeton University Press 1959, p89.

11   David Hughes, *The Star of Bethlehem Mystery*, Corgi, London 1981, p13.

12   David Hughes, *ibid.*

13   eg. Theodore H. Robinson, *The Gospel of Matthew*, Hodder and Stoughton, London 1927, pp7-8; F.W.Green, *The Gospel according to Saint Matthew*, S.C.M., London 1952, p31; J. C. Fenton, *The Gospel of St Matthew*, Pelican, London 1963, p46; Raymond E. Brown, *The Birth of the Messiah*, Chapman, London 1977, pp172-173.

14   David Hughes, *op. cit.* p228.

15   Werner Keller, *The Bible as History*, Hodder and Stoughton, London 1967, chapter 36 "The Star of Bethlehem", pp331-339.

16   The usual interpretation is that Saturn was the star of Israel, Jupiter the star of kingship, and Pisces the ruler of Palestine; eg., see C. G. Jung, *op. cit.*, p74.

17   David Hughes, *op. cit.* p227.

18   Werner Keller, *op. cit.* p336.

19   Giorgio de Santillana and Hertha von Dechend, *Hamlet's Mill*, Gambit, Ipswich 1969, pp244-245.

20   Giorgio de Santillana and Hertha von Dechend, *op. cit.* p59.

21   David R. Cartlidge and David L. Dungan, in *Documents for the Study of the Gospels*, Collins, London 1980, p178, refer to Virgil's *Eclogue IV* as "A Roman 'Messianic' Prophecy" and offer the following translation:

     The ultimate age of Cumae's song is now come!
     The great order is born anew from the line of the ages.
     The Virgin has now returned; Saturn's reign has returned;

Now a new offspring is sent from Heaven on High.
You alone grant favour at the birth of the boy by whom
the iron age
Shall cease and a golden race shall rise up on the world,
Only you, chaste Lucina; now your own Apollo
reigns.

22 Alan Oken, *Astrology: Evolution and Revolution*, Bantam, New York 1976, p28.

23 Alan Oken, *op. cit.* p22.

24 Vera W.Reid, *Towards Aquarius*, Aquarian, London 1969, pp60-61.

CHAPTER 6

1 C.H.Dodd, *The Interpretation of the Fourth Gospel*, Cambridge University Press 1965, pp236ff. For his full exposition see pp230-238.

2 Kenneth G. Cuming, *God and the New Age*, Courier, Tunbridge Wells. Articles based on a course of sermons delivered at the Church of Christ the Healer, Burrswood, p8.

3 See Bernard Capp, *Astrology and the Popular Press*, Faber and Faber, London 1979, chapter 5 "Almanacs and Religion" for a detailed account of the ambivalent attitude of the churches to astrology.

4 See the works of Michel and Françoise Gauquelin, *The Cosmic Clocks*, Peter Owen, London 1969; and *The Truth about Astrology* Hutchinson, London 1983. The most authoritative assessment of the Gauquelin's work is found in H. F. Eysenck and D. K. B. Nias, *Astrology, Science or Superstition?*, Penguin, London 1984.

5 Eric Newton and William Neil, *The Christian Faith in Art*, Hodder and Stoughton, London 1966, p31.

6 William Neil, *ibid.*

7 Gilbert Cope, *Symbolism in the Bible and in the Church*, S.C.M., London 1959, p37.

8 Gilbert Cope, *op. cit.* p35.

9 Edward Hulme, *Symbolism in Christian Art*, Blandford, Poole 1974, pp197-198.

10   Tertullian, *de Baptismo*, i; Gilbert Cope, *op. cit.* p37.
11   Gilbert Cope, *ibid.*
12   Gilbert Cope, *ibid.*
13   Herbert Whone, *Church, Monastery, Cathedral, A Guide to the Symbolism of Christian Tradition*, Compton Russell Element 1977, p73.
14   Herbert Whone, *op. cit.* p74.
15   Herbert Whone, *op. cit.* pp105-106.
16   John Michell, *City of Revelation*, Abacus, London 1973, p72.
17   Robert Lawlor, *Sacred Geometry*, Thames and Hudson, London 1982, p35.
18   Herbert Whone, *op. cit.* p112.
19   Robert Lawlor, *op. cit.* pp33-35.

CHAPTER 7

1   Lois Lang-Sims, *The Christian Mystery*, Allen and Unwin, London 1980, p68: "Many people have seen in this 'water bearer' a symbol of the dawn of the Aquarian age at the expiration of the Piscean, the fish being a recognised symbol of the Christ".
2   Peter Lemesurier, *The Gospel of the Stars*, Compton, Tisbury 1977, p43.
3   Vera W. Reid, *Towards Aquarius*, Aquarian, London 1969, p92.
4   Johannes Behm in Gerhard Kittel (ed.) *Theological Dictionary of the New Testament*, Eerdmans, Grand Rapids 1964, Vol 2, pp468-469. He gives the other theologically important uses of *ekcheō*, "pour out", as the violent killing of martyrs, eg. *Matt.* 23:35, *Acts* 22:20, *Rev.* 16:6 and the death of Jesus, *Mark* 14:24, *Matt.* 26:28, *Luke* 22:20.
5   Even when not referring explicitly to Pentecost, Paul still uses this metaphor to describe God's love which "has been poured into our hearts through the Holy Spirit", *Romans* 5:5. The close link which he makes between the Holy Spirit and 'pouring out' is also shown in *Titus* 3:5-6

where he speaks of Christ's "regeneration and renewal in the Holy Spirit, which he poured out on us". cf Johannes Behm, *ibid.*

6   For standard works on history and doctrine see Donald Gee, *Wind and Flame, The Pentecostal Movement*, Assemblies of God, Croyden 1976; John Thomas Nicol, *The Pentecostals*, Logos, Plainfield 1971; Vinson Synan, *The Holiness-Pentecostal Movement in the United States*, Eerdmans, Grand Rapids 1971; Walter J. Hollenweger, *The Pentecostals*, S.C.M., London 1972.

7   For standard works on history and doctrine see P.E.Shaw, *The Catholic Apostolic Church*, King's Crown, New York 1946; Roland A. Davenport, *Albury Apostles*, United Writers, London 1970.

8   Valentine Cunningham, "Texts and their Stories – 14", *Redemption Tidings*, October 1970, p3: "And the theological awareness makes Irvingism quite distinct from any isolated but perhaps ill-understood, occurrences of tongues among earlier revivalists; perhaps for the first time since Tertullian the participants knew precisely what was afoot". cf Ronald Knox, *Enthusiasm*, Oxford 1950, p551.

9   For a full account see C.Gordon Strachan, *The Pentecostal Theology of Edward Irving*, Darton, Longman and Todd, London 1973.

10   Edward Irving, *The Day of Pentecost or The Baptism with the Holy Ghost*, Baldwin and Craddock, London 1831.

11   W. H. Hudson, in his Introduction to Thomas Carlyle's, *Sartor Resartus* and *On Heroes and Hero Worship*, Everyman's Library, Dent, London 1967, pxii.

12   Thomas Carlyle, *op.cit.* p163.

13   Liz Greene, *Relating, An Astrological Guide to Living with Others on a Small Planet*, Coventure, Whitstable 1984 edn. p266.

14   Liz Greene, *op. cit.* p267.

15   Thomas Carlyle, *op. cit.* pp127-128.

16   *Everyman's Encyclopaedia*, Dent, London 1950, Vol 2, p68: "*Baphomet*, name of a mysterious idol with 2 heads, male and female, which the Templars were accused of

worshipping in secret with licentious rites. The word is a medieval form of Mahomet".

17   eg. I. Howard Marshall, *The Gospel of Luke*, Paternoster, Exeter 1978, p146: "For Luke himself the fulfilment of John's prophecy was doubtless the event of Pentecost (*Acts* 1:5) which was also a fulfilment of the prophecy of the outpouring of the Spirit in Joel 2:28; on this view Spirit and fire should not be regarded as alternatives, signifying salvation or judgment".

18   eg. G.E.P.Cox, *Saint Matthew*, S.C.M., London 1958, p35; H. Benedict Green, *Matthew*, Oxford University Press 1975, p63; William F. Arndt, *St Luke*, Concordia, St Louis 1956, p116; W.R.F.Browning, *Saint Luke*, S.C.M., London 1965, p56.

19   Sandra Levy, "The Importance of Leo in an Aquarian Age", *The Astrological Journal*, Summer 1984, p156.

20   Liz Greene, *op. cit.* p274.

21   Alan Oken, *Astrology: Evolution and Revolution*, Bantam, New York 1976, p33.

22   For: John L. Sherrill, *They Speak with other Tongues*, Hodder and Stoughton, London 1964. Against: John P. Kildahl, *The Psychology of Speaking in Tongues*, Hodder and Stoughton, London 1972. cf also James D.G.Dunn, *Baptism in the Holy Spirit*, S.C.M., London 1970.

23   eg. F. J. Foakes-Jackson, *The Acts of the Apostles*, Hodder and Stoughton, London 1931, p12: tongues are "allegorical of the future diffusion of the gospel to all nations".

24   eg. F. F. Bruce, *The Acts of the Apostles*, Tyndale, London 1962, p86: "The reversal of the curse of Babel is surely in the writer's mind".

25   Vera W.Reid, *op. cit* pp91-92.

26   J. W. Packer, *The Acts of the Apostles*, Cambridge University Press 1966, p28.

27   Ernst Haenchen, *The Acts of the Apostles*, Blackwell, Oxford 1971, p169.

28   Ernst Haenchen, *op. cit.* pp169-171.

29   Gilles Quispel, *The Secret Book of Revelation*, Collins, London 1979, p22.

30   Vera W.Reid, *op. cit.* p92.

31   Alan Oken, *op. cit.* p33.

32 Robert Maddox, *The Purpose of Luke – Acts*, Vandenhoeck and Ruprecht, Göttingen 1982, p137.
33 Alan Oken, *op. cit.* p31.
34 Alan Oken, *op. cit.* p39.
35 Kenneth G. Cuming, *God and the New Age*, Courier, Tunbridge Wells, p19.

CHAPTER 8

1 Jean-Jacques Rousseau, *The Social Contract*, chapter 1, "Man is born free, and everywhere he is in chains".
2 Martin Luther King, *Stride Towards Freedom: The Montgomery Story*, Harper and Row, New York 1958.
3 William Wilberforce, *Journal*, 28 October, 1787: "God Almighty has set before me two great objects: the suppression of the slave trade and the reformation of manners".
4 See Gustav Gutierrez, *A Theology of Liberation*, S.C.M., London 1983.
5 Alan Oken, *Astrology: Evolution and Revolution*, Bantam, New York 1976, p39.
6 Alan Oken, *op. cit.* p34.
7 C. G. Jung, *Aion*, Routledge and Kegan Paul, London 1959, quoted by Liz Greene, *Relating*, Coventure, Whitstable 1977, p273. Jung is of the opinion that Christ's birth coincided with the great conjunction of Saturn and Jupiter on 29 May, 7 B.C., ie in Gemini – the Twins: "One thinks involuntarily of the ancient Egyptian pair of hostile brothers". *op. cit.* pp77f.
8 Liz Greene, *op. cit.* p269.
9 Liz Greene, *op. cit.* p270.
10 Liz Greene, *op. cit.* pp275-276.
11 David Tame, *The Secret Power of Music*, Turnstone, Wellingborough 1984, p250.
12 Herbert Whone, *The Hidden Face of Music*, Gollancz, London 1974, p57.
13 David Tame, *op. cit.* p249.
14 Liz Greene, *op. cit.* p274.

15 George S. Hendry, *Theology of Nature*, Westminster, Philadelphia 1980, p78.

16 George S. Hendry, *op. cit.* p91: "But over all the strife there reigns harmony (*harmonia*, Heraclitus invented the word)".

17 Whether Christ was the incarnation of the specifically Heraclitean definition of the Logos has been the subject of enduring theological debate. Some scholars have maintained that St John was influenced more by late Hellenistic philosophy than by Heraclitus; others that he derived the concept more from the Old Testament doctrine of the Word and Wisdom of God and yet others that he got it from the Gnostics. There are also others who have suggested that certain Greek interpretations of the Logos, such as the Stoic, resembled the Hebrew to such an extent that they may be taken as being practically synonymous. For a comprehensive survey of all shades of opinion, see T. E. Pollard, *Johannine Christology and the Early Church*, Cambridge University Press 1970, pp6-15.

18 Justin Martyr, *Apologia* I 46, Henry Bettenson, Ed. *The Early Christian Fathers*, Oxford University Press 1969, p60.

19 Irenaeus, *Adversus Haereses*, IV 4:2, Henry Bettenson, *op. cit.* p76.

20 Eusebius, *Demonstratio Evangelica*, 4. 13. 2-3, in G. L. Prestige, *God in Patristic Thought*, S.P.C.K., London 1964, pp35-36.

21 See Paul Beasley-Murray, *The Cosmic Christ*, for a very detailed study of Paul's teaching on cosmic Christology. Labarum Publications, Dunbar, 1985.

22 G. L. Prestige, *op. cit.* p129.

23 T. E. Pollard, *op. cit.* p318.

24 Maurice Wiles, *The Christian Fathers*, Hodder and Stoughton, London 1966, p29.

25 Maurice Wiles, *op. cit.* p31.

26 Liz Greene, *op. cit.* pp264-265.

27 Alfred Douglas, *The Oracle of Change, How to Consult the I Ching*, Penguin, Harmondsworth 1977, p54. George S. Hendry points out the similarity between Heraclitus and Chinese philosophy of the same period, *op. cit.* p153:

"A remarkable parallel to the thought of Heraclitus is to be found in the ancient Chinese doctrine of yang and yin which developed in roughly the same period and in very similar circumstances."

APPENDIX

1   For an alternative interpretation of the sacred geometry of New Jerusalem, see John Michell, *City of Revelation*, Abacus, London 1972. His brilliant study is however, very difficult for those not acquainted with the gematria (the numerical correspondences to the Hebrew and Greek alphabets; it is from this that we get the word geometry) upon which his whole exposition is based. I offer my simpler version for those who know nothing of gematria or numerology. cf Oscar Cullmann, *Christ and Time*, S.C.M., London 1951, p188, for a similar model.

2   Robert Lawlor, *Sacred Geometry, Philosophy and Practice*, Thames and Hudson, London 1982, pp4-5.

3   For a comprehensive summary of the literature attributed to Hermes Trismegistus see C. H. Dodd, *The Interpretation of the Fourth Gospel*, Cambridge University Press 1953, chapter 2: "The person so called was represented as a sage of ancient Egypt, deified after his death as the Egyptian Hermes, that is, the god Thoth".

4   For a full explanation of this see F. F. Bruce's standard work, *The Spreading Flame*, Paternoster Press, Exeter 1958, p294.

5   T. S. Eliot, *Collected Poems*, Faber and Faber, London 1970 edn.,p191.

6   J. C. Cooper, *An Illustrated Encyclopaedia of Traditional Symbols*, Thames and Hudson, London 1978, p180.

7   Ros Herman, "Electrons get to the heart of the matter", *New Scientist*, 17 January, 1980.